The Ultimate Guide to Self Directed Investing & Retirement Planning

Control Your Financial Future, Self-Direct Your Investments, Create a Tax-Free "Bulletproof" Wealth Plan, & Live the Life You Want!

Jeff Barnes

Learn How to Beat the Tax Code and Retire In Style!

This publication is designed to provide accurate and authoritative information with regard to the subject matter covered. It is sold with the understanding that the publisher is not engaged in rendering legal, accounting, or other professional advice. If legal advice or other expert assistance is required, the services of a competent professional should be sought. The opinions expressed by the authors in this book are not endorsed by Best Seller Publishing® and are the sole responsibility of the author rendering the opinion.

Most Best Seller Publishing® titles are available at special quantity discounts for bulk purchases for sales promotions, premiums, fundraising, and educational use. Special versions or book excerpts can also be created to fit specific needs.

For more information, please write:
Best Seller Publishing®
1346 Walnut Street, #205
Pasadena, CA 91106
or call 1(626) 765 9750
Toll Free: 1(844) 850-3500
Visit us online at: www.BestSellerPublishing.org

CONTENTS

Acknowledgements

There are honestly too many people for me to fully acknowledge for the creation of this book. I don't know how many people I have learned from over the years in the fields of economics, finance, financial planning, business, and life in general. To say that I'm a self-made man would be a complete lie and absurdity. Mentors and coaches from various businesses in the past, as well as those I had in the Navy continue to inspire me even though it has been several years since I last spoke with them. Recent mentors and coaches have continued to prod me and guide me down this path which eventually culminated in the creation of this book, as well as a successful business and the realization of many dreams and goals.

Specifically, I must acknowledge the University of Washington Bothell MBA team and my peers for helping me to get through two years of continuous hardship, commuting, and regular trips on the road. Were it not for their guidance and support, I likely would have given up on earning my masters in the first place, and who knows where I would be now if I had done so. Their insights and camaraderie are truly second to none, and the culture that was fostered within those four walls continues to help me in my career years after completion of my courses.

Next I must acknowledge all of the contributors to this book. Each of these individuals has taught me a great deal about life, perseverance, and of course their chosen fields of study. These individuals have been a shining light for me to help see my true potential, as well as my ability to create and inspire others. Their ability to teach me in spite of all my stubbornness and hard headedness has been a truly wonderful example for me to follow in pursuit of my dreams.

Preface

This guide is meant only as educational material and is not intended to provide financial or legal advice. Nor is this book intended to give any retirement or investment advice. It is not intended to make or suggest any personal recommendation as to what any individual should or shouldn't choose regarding their personal financial strategy.

Each person needs to consult their own team of professionals and their own advisors in order to determine what actions are best for them. Therefore, I encourage you to seek professional advice from a knowledgeable advisor who fully understands all the concepts outlined in this guide, prior to proceeding with any investment or plan setup.

That being said, very few individuals will fully understand all the concepts outlined in this guide and it is therefore recommended to seek out professionals who have gone through this process before, prior to explaining or trying to reinvent the wheel with these types of investment tools.

I want to further stress that this book is not intended as a slight against the financial planning industry. I personally enjoy the process of working with clients helping them to realize their financial goals and dreams, and I know individuals who have chosen this profession feel the same way about their clients. For you financial advisors reading this book, understand this isn't intended to insult you, but rather think of this as a call to action for investors and large investment firms to wake up to the fact that there are better ways to go about the planning process than we have been conditioned to accept. The world ecosystem and economy has changed over the past fifty years drastically. Shouldn't our way of planning for retirement change as well.

Additional Resources for You

Since first writing this book, I took over the CEO role at Angel Investors Network. Since 1997 AIN has been helping create wealth and abundance through the power of entrepreneurship and investing, and now all of the resources in this book have been moved over to this platform.

Visit www.AngelNetwork.com/InnerCircle at any time when reading this book for various supplements and additional information to help you more thoroughly understand the concepts and ideas outlined in this book. We have provided several free resources, guides, videos, and audio recordings to supplement this book, as well as a really cool and easy tool for determining if you are ready for retirement.

As you read through this book, you are going to find yourself asking several questions that may not be written down on the pages but might be addressed in a webinar, interview, or additional training as a bonus for this book. I encourage you to visit the site above so you can access all of this great information and find out how you can get even more information and resources to help you on your path to successful retirement planning and investing.

Introduction

In December 2007, the United States entered a recession that lasted several years. All told, the US economy and its citizens lost $12.8 trillion over the course of just two years.[1] The full cost of this crisis is still being felt and continues to reverberate throughout the world economy as this writing occurs. During this period of confusion and angst, many people lost everything, including their homes, their vehicles, their jobs, and even their retirement accounts. Trillions of dollars of wealth evaporated in the blink of an eye and left so many people destitute. The crisis sparked uproar across the country and world, and many people began to revolt against Wall Street and the financial institutions that helped to fuel and cause this global meltdown. A rise of "Main St. vs. Wall St." emerged on the streets of cities and towns across America, and *Occupy Wall Street* became one of the largest demonstrations in the United States since Vietnam.

In light of the recent events, many people began to question the sanctity and safety of well-known investment firms, and also began to question the advice of their investment advisors. As someone who has been involved in the financial services and insurance industries for several years, I can say that I am just as enraged as any other individual out there who was harmed by this financial crisis. My wife and I

---

[1] Weise, K. (2012, Sep 17). Tallying the full cost of the financial crisis. *Business Week*, , 1. Retrieved from http://search.proquest.com/docview/1098180983?accountid=458

purchased a house at what we thought was a trough in the housing market in our area, only to later discover that our home price continued to slip by another 30% the year after we purchased it. I thought I understood real estate and financial markets pretty well given my education. However, as time soon showed, the complexities of our financial market went far beyond my basic understanding.

After being dealt a devastating blow from this financial crisis, I decided to reinvent myself and invest in my education and learn all I could about how markets work and how I could personally avoid such a disaster in the future. I went and got my MBA from the University of Washington, and read everything I could about economics and financial markets. In doing my research what I found was that one truism held throughout all the different aspects of investing: personal control and education are the only defense against negative external forces.

I learned about self-directed investing through various seminars I attended several years ago. At the time I was just beginning my real estate investing career, and learned there is a way that you could invest retirement plan money into real estate through the use of self-directed retirement plans. This piqued my interest at the time, but not much came of it because I didn't have very much money in any retirement plans to speak of. After the financial crisis however, I was bound and determined never to be one of the individuals that you will learn about in this book. My business partner and I started a company helping

2

people understand self-directed investments at a level that I think is unparalleled in the financial services industry. Each time we gain a new client, the same questions continue to plague their decisions to get a self-directed retirement plan. In light of that information, I decided to write this book to help others understand the entire self-directed retirement planning process, and why someone like you might want to have a truly self-directed retirement plan.

This book aims to help bridge the gap between education and personal control so that you can have both and begin to invest on your terms in such a way that a financial crisis or catastrophe in the future will not have such devastating effects as it did me. *The Ultimate Guide to Self-Directed Investing & Retirement Planning* is a book born out of necessity and circumstance. Necessity because the ways in which Americans earn a living and then retire has changed drastically over the past several decades, and new tools and techniques need to be employed in order to provide for successful retirement for individuals as well as the broader economy. Circumstances now dictate that there are better ways to invest your money and take personal control and responsibility of your finances. Bridging these two with the understanding of how you can invest your money for best returns and maximum tax savings is exactly what you're going to get out of this book.

I encourage you to take notes, write down ideas, and disagree with me at any point. It's important to understand that there are several ways to skin the proverbial cat, and no one way is the only solution. I hope you will find this information both helpful and useful, but more importantly I hope you begin to implement these tactics and strategies at your earliest convenience so you too can be prepared for a financial future full of uncertainty and volatility. Here's to a prosperous you!

This book is broken down into four parts. Each part builds upon the preceding section, and delivers even more in-depth information. For those who already understand self-directed investing and may even have your own self-directed plan, much of this may just be review. However, I encourage you to read through each section since they are rather brief, so that you fully understand the reasons for having a self-directed retirement plan, as well as the various pitfalls that you may encounter if you go about the self-directed retirement process incorrectly.

The first part talks about the history of retirement and how we got to this current stage of retirement evolution. The past is riddled with details many people fail to understand or neglect entirely, and as a result don't understand the entire reason for retirement planning to begin with. Risk management plays a huge role in the history of retirement, and our failure as a society to manage these risks has led to a financial crisis unparalleled throughout human history. Understanding more about the retirement planning history will help you to gain a better understanding of why it's important have the right type of retirement plan to begin with, as well as the right team in place to help you implement your plan.

Part two will walk you through the nuts and bolts of self-directed investing. Self-directed investing is simply a component of retirement planning that allows you to take direct control of your investments through proper planning and plan setup. Most people mistakenly think that they are already in control of their retirement plan as well as their investments within the plan. However, this section is going to provide much needed guidance on what self-directed investing is, as well as what you currently do not have in a retirement plan.

The third part of this book is going to explain all the pitfalls and "no-no's" of self-directed investing and retirement planning. There are six key factors that really led up to our financial crisis and the loss of the equivalent of our entire nation's gross domestic product (GDP) in the course of a year. I'm going to outline the six basic tenets of self-directed investing and retirement planning toward the end as well as the different circumstances that you do not want to find yourself in so that you are aware of what obstacles lay before you and your path for successful retirement planning and self-directed investing.

The final section of this book is going to outline various investment options that are available to self-directed investors. These investment options are not new, nor are they going to be strange elaborate investments that you've never heard of. In fact, many of these investment options are already available to you outside of your retirement plans. However, most people do not understand that you can actually invest in several different asset classes within your retirement plan. For that reason, I've enlisted the help of several experts to help me explain the various investment options available to you through self-directed investing. After all, what good is it to have a proper self-directed investment plan if you still choose the same terrible investments that landed us in the world's worst financial crisis since the Great Depression?

I've enjoyed writing this book and helping people along the way to a more secure financial future. I've worked with people who have absolutely nothing in terms of retirement all the way up through executives who could stop working tomorrow if they chose. Each of these people has had their eyes opened to the possibilities before them through proper education, planning, and implementation. I hope you too will be one of my successful case studies of people who have taken control of their financial future, and who will not let their fate be determined by faceless corporations on Wall Street looking out for their own best interests!

Part 1
The Way It Is

A Breath of Fresh Air

I was choking. I couldn't breathe. Water had completely filled my sinuses and my throat, and I could feel it forcing its way into my lungs.

I couldn't see either. My eyes were burning from the chlorine.

I could feel my heart beating in my throat and my ears.

Thump-thump. Thump-thump.

The worst part? I didn't have anywhere to go. Shooting to the surface wasn't an option since my lungs were pressurized from scuba air. However, my tanks were nowhere to be found. They had been ripped off me just seconds prior as if only attached by a single thread.

I fumbled around blindly searching for my breathing regulator, hose, or tank strap. Anything to help me find my tanks and regain my ability to breathe.

Nothing.

Up until this point I wasn't afraid. Now the fear was beginning to set in as I could feel myself being slowly asphyxiated by lack of oxygen. The burning sensation of the water inside my sinuses and eyes was nothing compared to the inability to take a breath.

I continued to search and reach for my tanks, trying to find anything, but all I could find was my buddy who was facing the same struggle. I searched and flailed and threw my arms, but still nothing.

My fins were gone. My tanks were gone. My regulator was nowhere to be found. My goggles were undoubtedly floating somewhere nearby but I couldn't see them.

Everything seemed lost...

"Jesus Barnes! That's one helluva chicken head move," came the hysterical comment from one of my instructors in the back of the room, as my head was bouncing back and forth on the video in an obvious struggle to regain my ability to breathe.

We were watching footage of what many of us in the class affectionately referred to as "Shark Week": several days of scuba diver training in Pearl Harbor Hawaii where our limits and abilities were tested underwater by removing all of our gear and forcing us to find a way to save ourselves without putting us or anyone else in danger. Failure to pass through this week or any other test administered throughout the five-week intensive program resulted in getting sent back to the fleet without your diver pin. I had tried for so long to get into this school, and I wasn't about to let something as silly as not being able to breathe stop me from getting my pin!

The easiest and quickest way to be completely disqualified was to attempt to shoot to the surface in fear when you're not able to breathe. Trying to go to the surface in a pool is easy for most people. When your lungs are pressurized with 3000 pound air from a scuba tank, shooting to the surface like that could result in immediate death.

The purpose of these "shark attacks" was to see how we would handle ourselves under pressure when no one else was around to save us. The last thing you want to do was exhibit any amount of fear which resulted in immediate disqualification.

Up until this point I hadn't needed any assistance throughout the training. I wasn't the fastest swimmer or runner, nor could I hold my breath the longest, but I damn sure was determined to pass no matter what it took. So many people had their doubts about my abilities, but I wasn't going to give into their condescending laughs and mocking gestures if I returned empty-handed.

Now the Navy isn't entirely harsh. In fact it's still one of the safest organizations I've ever worked with in my life. Since they don't want you to die, especially on their watch, they have safety divers stationed right next to you with an extra breathing apparatus to help you in the event you do run into any difficulties. I now found myself in this situation, having my regulator ripped from my mouth as I was taking a deep breath, forcing me to swallow a mouthful of pool water.

By this time jumping to the surface was not even a consideration for me. I'd made it through three weeks of intensive training so far, and knew what I needed to do was gesture for air. I took my hand and made the universal gesture for "stop talking" by horizontally slicing it back

11

and forth across my throat, then tapping my lips profusely to let my safety diver know I needed air immediately. All was saved, though not with a little bit of humiliation.

As we were sitting in our graduation ceremony watching these videos, the whole ordeal looked incredibly silly and seemed to have gone by without any issue. However, in those moments when I was gasping for breath and couldn't find my equipment, it was anything but silly.

That experience, and many more throughout my life have helped me realize one very important aspect of living that I've formed into my own personal philosophy: education, training, and responsibility have no substitutes.

If I had been tested like this on the very first day of my training, there is no doubt I would've failed immediately and returned back to my submarine to see the looks of disgust and frustration on my fellow submariner's faces. Lucky for me, I was involved in a world-class training program that built one upon one to that moment so that I had no fear of failure.

Unfortunately, this same type of training is not available to most individuals growing up. This is especially true in the realm of personal finance. Most people live at home with their parents or guardians until they are about 18 years old, maybe 22 if they go to college, and are then thrust out into the world and told to sink or swim. Very little formal education or training is ever gone into preparing people for investing or personal finance, and as a result many of our Millennial's and Echo-boomer's are completely underwater financially with very little hope of ever returning to the surface safely.

The purpose of this book is to help individuals understand the realm of investing in finance on a very basic level, and then couple that with the idea or philosophy of personal responsibility. The truth of the matter is that the world of retirement and investing has changed significantly over the past several decades, yet our understanding and education on the topic has not improved enough. Markets are incredibly intertwined and difficult to understand, and therefore so many people have given up hope of ever understanding how to invest or plan for their future, and instead hand over the reins to someone who may know only a trifling amount more.

Let me be your guide as you wander through the world of personal finance, investing, and retirement planning. I promise you that this book will not make you an expert in all things investing or personal finance related, but it will open the door to realm of possibilities that you are otherwise unaware of. Additionally, if you take me up on the opportunities throughout this book to get more information and training, I will continue to be there to help you along every step of the path.

Because let's face it, sometimes taking the easy route and shooting to the surface can be the worst possible decision of your life. Instead, it's better to have someone there to lend you a hand and give you a chance to breathe again on your own, and in so doing, maybe save your life!

A Warning About Self-Directed Plans!

Everywhere you look these days people are contradicting themselves. If you watch FOX News to get a story then turn the channel and watch CNN ten minutes later, you're bound to get two completely opposing and different stories about the exact same topic. Such is the world that we live in these days. Technology and communication channels abound, and with that, misinformation can be fed to individuals at a much faster pace than ever before. It is for this very reason that I decided to write this book. Everywhere I looked in doing my research I found misinformation, misguided individuals, and several different stories that did not corroborate the facts. Even when doing my own research I had to adjust my message simply because new information, or rather better information, came to light. In this book you will hear several stories and examples about individuals who were led astray by either uninformed advisors, or simply because they tried to screw the rules in hopes that no one would catch them. One such individual attempted to purchase a business using his retirement plan, which is completely legal, but then wanted to get reimbursed for some of his out-of-pocket expenses. To most people who have not spent a lot of time dealing with retirement plans, this is completely legitimate. If you start a business then why shouldn't you get reimbursed for some of the expenses required to get the business running? However, the rules change somewhat once you begin dealing with self-directed retirement plans, and it's important for you to understand that there are a lot of rules and regulations around retirement plans in general. Take for example two individuals who ran an extremely successful business purchased through their retirement plans, but eventually sold the business netting them several hundred thousand dollars in profit only to find out later that a certain little piece of paper they signed caused all their profits to be taxed as ordinary income! Imagine the frustration and pain these investors had to go through when they realized that not only did they have to pay penalties and fines, but they had to pay back taxes on income that they were assuming was going to be tax free!

Horror stories like these abound. This book is designed to help you avoid becoming one of them. That being said, it's important that you first read through the book to get basic information about how the effects of retirement plans and retirement planning in general can help you to succeed in the world of finance. Once you've completed that, it's important to surround yourself with like-minded individuals and savvy advisors who will guide you down the path of least resistance. I have made every attempt during the research portion of this book to ensure that all the facts are current, up-to-date, and correct. However I can make absolutely no guarantees about the future laws or rules that might be passed by Congress or any other individuals within the bureaucracy that is the IRS. Additionally, what we are going to discuss it somewhat of a gray area for many individuals. Some folks will try to push the envelope a little bit too far and it will eventually burst, resulting in court cases, fines, penalties, and their names plastered all over the front page of the newspaper. I urge you to seek out proper advice and guidance prior to venturing down the path of self-directed investing and alternative retirement planning. The book is meant as a guide, not the end all, be all for advice or legal matters. Just the way a tour guide in a foreign land shows you what parts of town are good and what back-alleys to avoid, but can't keep you from going down those bad alleys, so too can this book guide you in the right direction and help you make wise decisions, but can't stop you from making poor and sometimes illegal choices. This book will also help you to ask the right questions when you seek out a proper advisor. The last thing you want to do is get to the end of this book, assume that you know everything about self-directed investing and retirement planning, and attempt to go out and set up a plan and invest on your own. As you will find in many of the examples found in this book, people who have done that have suffered dearly and wish they could retrace their steps and start over correctly. You are starting out correctly. Just make sure you finish on the same footing.

What is Retirement?

The term retirement brings up some seriously negative connotations to me. I want to bring that up right from the get-go because I want you to understand how I feel about actual retirement. In my opinion, no one should ever retire…at least not entirely. Now I don't want you think that my head is in the clouds and think everyone is working at their passion and loving every single day of their job. I know that's not nearly the case, otherwise we would have much more productive society- everyone walking around with smiles on their face and the sun would always be shining! That's not what I mean at all.

In some cases, retirement has been defined as "a complete withdrawal from the labor force". In other areas it's also been referred to as a complete withdrawal from society. In my opinion no one really wants to withdraw from society, and no one really wants to stop being productive. We may desire to no longer be employed at our current job or doing the same things we don't enjoy day in and day out, but we never really want to stop being productive citizens. Most people who stop being productive at anything just wither away and disappear into nothingness. If that's really what you want, then I suggest that you stop reading this right now because I'm not going to be able to help you.

Instead, I want to paint a new picture on the term "retirement". I will continue to use the word retirement simply because it's a colloquial term that everybody understands in today's society, but if I had my way we would change the term altogether. I think that after a lifetime of meaningful work and productivity one should be able to pursue their passion without any remorse or guilt. I've heard the term *"Freedom Day"* used, and I think that is very close to the mark for many people. However, many individuals truly do work at their passion and really enjoy what they do, so technically they should already be free correct? I will discuss the history of retirement here shortly, but suffice it to say that the term retirement will continue to be used throughout this book simply in reference to the normal retirement age of 65, or 59 ½ years old for qualified plans, or to reference what the IRS calls qualified or "retirement" plans. Many individuals will "retire" long before that, but for the purposes of this book, I really need to hone in on what the government considers retirement, and how that plays into the various types of retirement plans, otherwise known as qualified plans.

So how did we come to this idea of retirement anyways? Actually, retirement was a progression over the course of many generations. During the Middle Ages many households did not part ways when sons and daughters came of age, but rather continued to live on the same farms and facilities and use the same resources they had available to them growing up. When the patriarch of the family ended up getting a little bit too old to actively work on and maintain the farm and ranch, the next in line would generally take over duties and provide assistance for the aged parents.[2] As time pressed on and technology evolved, we began to see changes in how households progressed and care for one another. During the Industrial Revolution, new factories and the promise of higher pay lured many young workers off farms and into urban areas.

Throughout the 1800s, Europe was experiencing massive growth in its industrial facilities and needed ways to lure workers to the factories and off these rural ranches and farms. Otto von Bismarck, the first German Chancellor, created the first version of the modern welfare state to help him win the hearts and mind of his people so that he and Prince Wilhelm I could unify Germany for the first time in history. What Bismarck suggested was that *". . . those who are disabled from work by age and invalidity have a well-grounded claim to care from the state."[3]* Ironically, Bismarck implemented this system as a revolt against socialism, even though he would later be considered a Socialist for creating such a system. The goal was simple: show Germans that if they stood by their country and the companies they created that the government would take care of them when they could no longer work

---

[2] Plakans, Andrejs 1989 "Stepping Down in Former Times: A Comparative Assessment of Retirement in Traditional Europe." In David Kertzer and K. Warner Schaie, eds., *Age Structuring in Comparative Perspective.* Hillsdale, N.J.: Erlbaum.

[3] Social Security Administration (n.d.). *Social Security History.* Retrieved 2014, from http://www.ssa.gov/history/ottob.html

and be productive.

This same idea came of age in the United States approximately 60 years later. President Franklin D. Roosevelt organized the Committee on Economic Security (CES) in 1934 in an effort to address the problems of old age in poverty in the United States.[4] From there, we got the Social Security Act of 1935 which still lives on today with Social Security insurance, disability insurance, and other benefits many people don't realize. The goal of the Social Security Act was to provide a means for elderly workers to leave the workforce without having to worry about the costs associated with living. The goal was to help people leave the workforce and not be so dependent upon a job for a wage. We will talk more about Social Security in a future chapter, but suffice it to say Social Security only did us so much good.

In a continual effort to win skilled labor and talent to companies, many organizations created a defined benefit plan, also known as a pension plan. These types of plans helped to ensure workers were going to be able to live well into retirement age even after they were no longer able to work for a factory or facility. The goal here too was rather simple: invest a certain portion of each worker's wage into a plan that will continue to grow over the years and then when the employee stopped working, they would receive a monthly stipend until the day

---

[4] HARDY, M. A., & SHUEY, K. (2001). Retirement. In *Encyclopedia of Sociology* (2nd ed., Vol. 4, pp. 2401-2410). New York: Macmillan Reference USA

they died in order to help support their lifestyle. Again, this is a very good and noble plan and worked very well for very long period of time. One tenet of these plans that made them viable was that people would stop working somewhere around age 65, but would only live for 5-10 years thereafter. This meant 40 years of work for a company covered about ten years of retirement. This was an easy cost for companies to manage, and worked well for a couple of generations.

Unfortunately, the baby boom after the Second World War created a massive shift in demographics that none of these companies and government agencies were able to predict. As a result, we went from an era with fewer retirees compared to the number of workers in the labor force to a new era where more people are retiring than are entering the workforce. This tips the scales drastically in favor of the retirees. Since many pension plans are underfunded, including Social Security, many of the retirees are living on borrowed time and wages from current employees, not their own contributions. In fact, recent study showed that 94% of pension plans out there today are still underfunded.[5] This represents a major issue for many companies and municipalities, and also represents a huge and significant cost for these companies.

This is why in 1974 Gerald Ford signed into law the Employee

---

[5] Sullivan, J. (2013). 94% of pension plans underfunded: Wilshire. *AdvisorOne.*

Retirement Income Security Act otherwise known as ERISA. This act created what we now know as defined contribution plans. These plans are discussed at length in this book and include such plans as 401(k)s and individual retirement accounts or IRAs. What this did was it shifted the burden from employers to employees to fund the employees' retirement incomes. Unfortunately as with any tectonic shift, the effects of this legislation were not felt until many years later when it became brutally apparent that Americans were underfunding their retirement by a significant amount. It's akin to a tidal wave hitting the Asian coast several days after an earthquake rocks the Western United States. What starts as a very small swell and surge in the ocean erupts into a force that no one predicted, yet became strong enough to bring down a nuclear power plant and an entire economy!

In the coming chapters I am going to discuss the various types of retirement plans that most people understand. However there are very subtle differences within these different types of plans, as well as how they are administered. It's important to understand how these plans are administered so that you can effectively utilize the tools that you have at your disposal to maximize your own investment returns and therefore your ability to retire with the amount of money you want, need, desire, and are hoping for to fund your lifestyle. Don't ever let anyone tell you that these tools and tactics cannot be done. We have several clients who have already implemented the strategies you are about to learn, and many have been able to shave years off of their working careers to retire early. Read on to see how you can become one of these individuals.

The Retirement Planning Process

Before we dive into the nuts and bolts of creating a successful retirement plan, you first need to understand what the retirement planning process is. After all, there's no point in knowing what an engine is and how it works if you don't know what the heck it is supposed to do, right? So, let's start with the broad picture of the retirement (and financial) planning process so that you can fully understand how self-directed investing fits into your plan.

Let's lead in with a story about a hypothetical couple, Joe and Breanne Johnson. The two met in college during some invigorating study about the principles of macroeconomics. Exciting, right?!? Well, the two hit it off like most couples do, dated for a couple of years, and after they both got their careers started, decided to get married. All was well in Joe-Anne world, and the couple was enjoying newly wedded bliss when something unplanned happened…Breanne got pregnant. All went well through the first trimester, then another surprise…twins! (Yes, those types of surprises still do happen)

This changed things for Joe and Breanne. They weren't planning on having two children at the same time, nor did they think it would happen so soon. After all, they were both only 26 years old and had just started eking out a living together. Now they were going to have two extra mouths to feed, less sleep then they ever realized, and a significantly reduced income. After all, child care was about equivalent to Breanne's salary, so she wanted to stay home with the children while they were infants. This left the Johnson's with a serious situation on their hands, and one that they weren't too well prepared for.

They decided to seek out professional help, and started asking around about good financial planners they could talk to about their situation. The first question that came to Joe's mind when he started thinking about the babies on the way, his wife's health, reducing their income down to a single person's, maternity leave for his wife and himself, and all the other myriad issues that were about to pounce upon him, was "Where the hell do I turn for help?!?" It's a fair question.

After all, there isn't one person who handles all of those questions who has "credentials" in every area. Joe could ask his CPA about tax implications of having two babies and losing his wife's income. What would their tax bill be? How can he maximize his earned income to support the family?

He could turn to his Human Resources (HR) department to get advice on health insurance and possible paternity leave, but they couldn't help with answering his wife's maternity leave questions since she worked elsewhere.

State agencies could help Joe and Breanne with Family and Medical Leave (FMLA) information, but that would just raise even more questions about short term and long term disability.

They could of course talk to their doctor about health concerns, diets, dos and don'ts of pregnancy and post-partum, but they couldn't get answers to their medical bills from the doctor. To get that information, they needed to turn to hospital administrators and their health insurance company.

Then he had really big questions about how he could support his family long term, especially if Breanne wanted to stay home with the kids. How much money did Joe need to bring home each pay period to support their lifestyle? What type of insurance would he need to cover his new pride and joy if anything happened to him? And then there's the even longer term: buying cars for the family vehicle, school supplies, cars for the kids when they get older, college funding, paying for weddings! Holy crap, what just happened!?!

Isn't that how most parents start to think when they become parents for the first time? As dads, we act totally cool and collected on the outside because our wife is one step from being a hormonal Hulk if we step out of line, right? Or maybe she is scared and needs our support? either way, dads try to act cool; like they have their crap together and figured out.

The truth is that Joe, and all dads at this point, really started to freak out. What was just a blissful honeymoon, dancing, partying, hanging out with the guys, etc. just turned into a WTF moment of panic! Now he really has to man up and figure out how to take care of his family.

Joe was a very bright young man, and after reading some information online and in books (like this one!) he decided he needed a financial planner who could help him get things in order and start to help them both plan their lives so they could continue to have the same standard of living even though they were doubling the size of their family.

But this begs the question, "What is financial planning anyways?" This is another good question, and one that isn't easily answered. However, the Certified Financial Planner Board has defined financial planning in this way:

The *Standards of Professional Conduct* (*Standards*) defines financial planning as "the process of determining whether and how an individual can meet life goals through the proper management of financial resources. Financial planning integrates the financial planning process with the financial planning subject areas.

There are six steps to the financial planning process:

Establishing and defining the client-planner relationship

Gathering client data including goals

Analyzing and evaluating the client's current financial status

Developing and presenting recommendations and/or alternatives

Implementing the recommendations

Monitoring the recommendations[6]

Well, what does that all mean?

The definition I found to be the most meaningful comes from a financial planner who has been in the business for over 40 years now, Jack Blankinship. He was quoted in the Journal of Financial Planning in 2001 defining the process as "a way to bring the many divergent aspects of a client's financial life together into a coordinated, integrated whole".[7] To me, this means that you are trying to find every available resource in a person's life that they can use to further their circumstances and lot in life with the least amount of confusion and frustration possible.

Remember all those people Joe and Breanne needed to consult to get answers to their burning questions? Well, a good financial planner who fully understands this holistic approach could help them through an objective lens. I talk in other sections of this book about how certain types of planners do not, or cannot due to license restrictions, help people in a holistic manner. Instead, they have various products and services they can provide, but it may not be enough to help a person in

---

[6]For CFP® Professionals. (2014, June 3). *Financial Planning FAQ*. Retrieved July 2, 2014, from http://goo.gl/3IihGE

[7] Lee, S. A. (2001). What is financial planning anyway? *Journal of Financial Planning, 14*(12), 36-46.

all these different areas.

Below is a chart that will help you understand all the ways in which a financial planner can help a person to construct a good financial and retirement plan. Although the Johnsons aren't quite ready to retire, much of what they are going to discuss with a good planner will help them to start planning for that eventual day when they want to send the kids off to college, buy an RV, and travel around the country worry-free. Well, sort of worry-free…I don't think anyone with children can ever truly be without worry, can they?

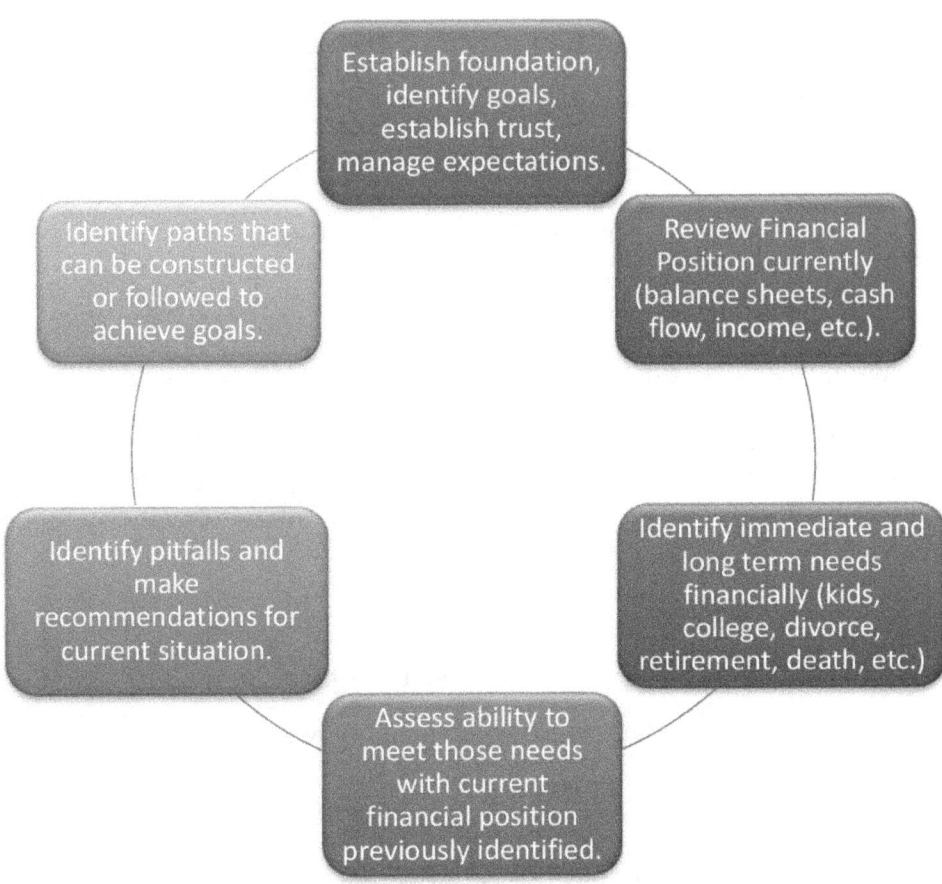

This should help you to understand what financial planning, and subsequently, what financial planners *should* be doing for you. I say "should" because not all planners have the best of intentions. Some just want your money and your business, but the good ones, the honest and ethical ones, will only help you if they can and know how.

Okay, so now Joe has decided to sit down with a certified financial planner (CFP) who only takes clients on a flat-fee basis. He found out that planners who only offer a couple products and services for commissions didn't answer all the questions he had, and found a good planner who was willing to help for a fixed hourly rate.

But now what can he expect to get out of his meeting with his new planner?

Well, below are the areas financial planners can help with, though not all will have expertise in each area. Additionally, many financial planners will have a team in place who can answer very specific questions on specific topics that they themselves cannot answer.

I have grouped the areas of focus into four key areas where most trained planners can help or advise clients. Again, not all will have a good foundation in these areas, but they should be able to help you find the right person for your situation.

Retirement Plans	• IRA's • 401(k) accounts • Mutual Funds • Self-directed accounts • Pensions • 403(b) accounts
Investment Planning (non-retirement)	• Stock Broker • Mutual Funds • Alternative Assets • Asset Manager • Broker/ Dealer services • Financial Analysis
Taxation	• Tax analysis for investing • Generally do not prepare tax returns • Answer tax questions related to qualified plans • Can answer basic questions about taxation of investments
Insurance	• Life Insurance • Health • Disability • Long Term Care • Auto/home/ property • Liability

Don't worry, we will cover all of these aspects later in the book. For now, just understand that the financial and retirement planning process can take a great deal of time when done correctly, but you get a lot out of it. As with anything, you get out in proportion to what you put in. Therefore, a good financial planner will ask you for more documentation and information than you ever thought you'd need to divulge. This is necessary so that your financial planner has a completely holistic view of your financial situation, as well as where you want to go. I'd suggest that you don't do any work with a planner who doesn't ask what your goal and purpose is for getting a planner. It doesn't make sense to start building a map if you don't know where you want to go, does it?

Back to the Johnsons. Now that they have a planner in place, they are ready to begin. A few things they discussed are:

- How much money will they likely need to sustain their current standard of living?
- What types of risks do they need to consider now that they are going to have less income and two children?
- How are they going to afford their long term financial goals such as buying a house, buying new cars, funding education, etc.?
- What types of investment options do they have available and how will that help them achieve their goals?
- What prospects do they have for retirement, even though it may be four decades away?

- Do they have a budget that shows them where the money is coming from and going to?

These types of questions are highlighted through insurance, financial, and lifestyle needs questionnaires financial planners provide. After providing documentation and answering the questions, the planner will have a good idea of what the Johnsons need, where they are now, and where they want to be.

The next step is to build a road map for success. This is where many planners will earn their fees, or leave the Johnsons wanting. Either they are going to have a fully fledged game plan outlining the pitfalls, risks, opportunities, and gaps, or they are just going to make recommendations in areas they can help. In either case, the Johnsons should feel comfortable that they are better prepared to handle the two bundles of joy on the way, and should hopefully have the majority of their financial, insurance, and tax questions answered.

During the process, Joe and Breanne found one thing very intriguing- the planner wanted to help them set up a retirement plan. This was intriguing to them because, as I mentioned, they were young and just started their careers. Why the heck do they need to plan for four decades hence when they don't even know if they want cloth or disposable diapers yet? The answer is quite simple, and it comes back to Einstein. Yes, simple *and* Albert Einstein!

You see, Einstein is (supposedly) quoted as having said "compound interest is truly one of the greatest inventions of our time!" Well, with a nod to Einstein, I don't think it's truly a great "invention" at all. You see, Mother Nature has been using compounding for quite some time through the conception and growth process of every living organism in this world. After all, you and I both started as a single cell, yet now we have several trillion cells making up our bodies, minds, and everything therein.

However, you didn't start as a trillion-celled organism, but rather became one over time. The same is true for retirement planning- it is a process of compounding money over the course of several years. This effect is amplified when you consider the tax-free or tax deferred status of retirement plans. The Johnsons received information about retirement planning early on because they have the advantage of time on their side right now. Retirement planning is the act of taking the financial planning process and forecasting it over the course of an individual's life and beyond.

I want you to stop thinking of retirement planning as getting 50% of your current income starting on the day you quit your job or turn 65. Instead, I want you to start thinking of retirement as a new stage in your life where you stop trading hours for dollars and instead start letting money do the heavy lifting for you. Through proper retirement planning you will have a true force of nature on your side- that of compounding interest. This is also known as the time value of money, or TVM for short. We will cover that topic shortly, but first, you need to understand where your current advisor fits in with the entire planning process.

The Financial Planner

If you're a financial planner reading this book, try not to get too offended when you read this chapter. What I'm about to say is frustrating and borderline hurtful for some people, but it's the honest truth, which is all I want you to have at this point!

A financial planner is a person who has made it their life's mission to help others lead more successful and financially free lives. The goal of the planner, as stated earlier, is to provide a holistic view of one's current and future financial needs and somehow create a game plan to meet those needs. Unfortunately, planners are susceptible to the same idiosyncrasies you and I are, and don't always plan accordingly. What I mean is, shit happens in our lives that we can't adequately prepare and plan for!

I have an engineering and math background from my days in the Navy, and then moved onto the risk management field. While in each of these areas I dabbled in financial planning and wanted to know all the ins and outs of the process and how the industry worked. I kept getting frustrated with my prospects and clients because I couldn't figure out why they didn't want to follow my recommendations when they seemed so logical!

What I, and so many other planners didn't understand was human psychology and sales. You see, the two fields are very closely related, and great salespeople are also great at understanding psychology and using that to their advantage. Let me give you an example. Think about the Johnsons from our previous chapter. They had a lot of challenges coming up, and you and I can see them after having read that chapter. However, how many people do you know who are blind to the challenges they face? How many people would have ignored the impending decisions until it was too late?

Perhaps you are someone who has ignored warning signs, advice, and put off decisions until the proverbial tomorrow in hopes of having better information on which to act? I know that was, and to an extent still is, my thought process.

"I can't plan for tomorrow without knowing what the future will bring, so I'm not going to plan right now for an unknown tomorrow!"

That was literally my thought process because as I said, I have an engineering mind. I needed *perfect information* (if there is such a thing) before I could make a choice on anything. In the Navy we call that "nuking it out"; trying to get so much information that you paralyze yourself with the details. This is also known as "analysis paralysis".

The problem with this thought process is that if we continue to put off our plan, then we fail to have anything in place for our goals when we need it. This is especially true of money and financial security.

This is where the financial planner comes in. The goal of the planner is to help you understand various life events and challenges you will face, and help you to prepare for them financially. In many cases, this process starts with a personal financial income statement, balance sheet, and cash flow analysis, also known as a financial analysis. These numbers are then projected and compared with your financial goals, and the process is to somehow match your current situation with your future financial goals.

The process then moves into the "risk mitigation" phase where insurances of all shapes and sizes are recommended. As a risk manager, I am routinely looking at potential risks and setbacks, and therefore I can't blame financial planners for focusing on potential losses first. However, the issue with this is that most people are coming to a financial planner with little or no wealth, spendable cash, or clue as to how to make more money. Therefore, when the first step of the planner is to buy insurance that a person is already convinced they don't need, the planner faces an uphill battle, and the customer faces an awkward moment of having to "politely" remove themselves from the room or relationship.

This isn't good for anyone, and doesn't solve any problems. Of course insurance is absolutely necessary to defend against uncertain loss, and we will cover that in a later section. However, the goal that most people have on their minds is to create wealth, not protect against an unknown loss. That is of course until they experience a loss and wonder how they're ever going to recover!

Most financial planners truly are passionate about their clients; passionate about creating wealth for families; passionate about helping others. However, their passion is very often overshadowed by the fact that they are attempting to sell a product that people don't think they need. Additionally, many planners earn commissions on the products they provide, and are prohibited from offering certain products or services because they are hampered by their licenses or company offerings and regulations. The Securities & Exchange Commission (SEC) also prohibits wandering outside the lines.

This is why what you are going to read in the remainder of this book is such a departure from what you might already know about financial and retirement planning and investing. Most planners are sales people, whether they care to admit it or not. I am a sales person, but (at least currently) I don't earn my income through a commission. I prefer a fee-based and performance based approach to creating revenue. It is against my moral code to earn a living purely on a commission-based incentive program.

Think about it: I'm going to sell you a service that will benefit me only if I sell it. True, it should benefit you too, but what if there was something else that could benefit you more? If I'm not able to advise on, or offer a product or service, even though I know it is a better solution for you, aren't I doing you a disservice?

I do believe most financial planners have the best of intentions

44

about what they do and offer. I also believe many of them love the companies they work for and will continue to sing its praises. However, that is where I differ. I prefer to provide sound advice and guidance based on something larger than my own company's limited offerings and services, and if I believe you will benefit by going elsewhere or seeking out a second opinion, then I think that is in the best interest of my clients. That is why I call myself a *Financial Strategist & Consultant* rather than a planner or advisor. My beliefs are different, and I'm guessing that if you choose to continue reading, yours are too!

What is the Time Value of Money?
The True Secret of Wealth Building

I just took you on a short journey through a young couple's life where they started thinking about retirement before their babies were born. Why did I do that? Well, quite simply because I need you to understand that the "retirement planning" process doesn't have a start or end date. It is a perpetual and evolving process in which you sit down and review where you are and where you want to be in the future. You also have to start asking how you are going to get there and get access to the types of investments that will take you where you need to be.

For now, I want to go back to a term I introduced in a previous chapter- the time value of money (TVM). The TVM is a term used in the financial and business world to mean that basically time is money. Yes, we all know the cliché that time is money, but I am going to show you how to actually put a dollar value on your time! Actually, I'm going to show you how to put a lot of dollars into time.

The concept of the time value of money is that a single dollar today isn't worth the same as a single dollar next year. In fact, it holds true for any currency- Pesos, Yuan, Euros, Pounds, etc. The fact is that time changes the value of currency, or money. That is exactly what the time value of money is- the change in value of money over the course of time. In order to determine what the time value of money is, you need to understand that there are factors involved in changing monetary values over time. Some of these factors include:

- **Inflation** - this phenomenon is caused by the fact that supply and demand of goods and services fluctuates over time and therefore the prices of these goods and services will tend to rise (or fall in the case of deflation) in monetary value. Now of course that is an over-simplification of the process since the central banks of the world tinker with our money supply to adjust inflation rates, but the premise remains.

- **Investment Return Rates**- in the calculation for TVM, the investment return rate has the same effect as the inflation rate, though in this case the result can have a positive impact on finances rather than a negative impact. I will show you very soon how the investments you choose will have a varying degree of risk and return, and therefore you will make money faster in certain types of investments rather than others.

- **Time**- the longer time horizon you have, the greater your return can be overall. This is why we started with an example of a young couple, not someone ready to kick the bucket. Their time horizon is going to have a huge impact on their overall return.

- **Periodic Payments**- the more you invest today, the more it will grow into tomorrow. Most people can't put $1,000,000 into an investment on day one, so payments into the plan will make the entire process manageable and work for you. Even starting out with almost nothing can add up over time.

One way of visualizing the time value of money is through an old question about receiving money: If I offered you $250,000 today, or offered you one penny ($0.01) today and doubled it every day for 30 days, which would you choose?

Now, on the face of this (if you've never been posed that question before) you would opt for $250,000 up front, right? After all, that can buy you a house, pay off your debt, buy a yacht, send you around the world, pay for your kid's college, or any number of things, right? (Well, maybe not as much after taxes, but that's a different story altogether!☺)

Well, let's look at how that second scenario would play out:

Day	Amount Paid
1	$ 0.01
2	$0.02
3	$0.04
4	$0.08
5	$0.16
6	$0.32

7	$0.64
8	$1.28
9	$2.56
10	$5.12
11	$10.24
12	$20.48
13	$40.96
14	$81.92
15	$163.84
16	$327.68
17	$655.36
18	$1,310.72
19	$2,621.44
20	$5,242.88
21	$10,485.76
22	$20,971.52

23	$41,943.04
24	$83,886.08
25	$167,772.16
26	$335,544.32
27	$671,088.64
28	$ 1,342,177.28
29	$ 2,684,354.56
30	$ 5,368,709.12

So, now you can see how doubling even the smallest amount of money every day for 30 days can yield amazing results- $5,368,709 worth of amazing results! Well, that is effectively what the Time Value of Money is- increasing your investment over and over again! Now, obviously doubling your money every day, or even every year isn't feasible, but the premise is still the same.

Let's get to a real world example using a few different interest rates as a tester. Let's say that you have the opportunity to earn 1%, 3%, 6%, and 12% on your investments. How will that stack up over time? Using the Johnsons as an example, let's say they could only afford to invest $3,000 per year ($250 per month), did that for ten years, and then retired in 40 years. Here's how that looks:

Return % and Final Value				
Year	1%	3%	6%	12%
1	$3,000	$3,000	$3,000	$3,000
5	$15,303	$15,927	$16,911	$19,059
10	$31,387	$34,392	$39,542	$52,646
15	$32,988	$39,869	$52,917	$92,781
20	$34,670	$46,219	$70,814	$163,511
25	$36,439	$53,581	$94,766	$288,162
30	$38,298	$62,115	$126,818	$507,841
35	$40,251	$72,008	$169,711	$894,989
40	$42,304	$83,478	$227,111	$1,577,276

Remember, in this scenario, we stopped investing altogether in year 11, and just let compound interest do the heavy lifting from there. Below is an example of how continuing to put that same amount in over time drastically changes the outcome. The point is to never stop investing for your future!

Now, what you should notice is that you're not just getting a 12x return from the 1% to the 12% jump ($42,304 x 12 = $507,648). Instead, you're getting a 12x return multiplied by the life of your investment, which turns out to be 37 times greater for the 12% return than for the 1% return. This is how the time value of money can really shape your financial future and help you to see how you can live the life you've desired every day you punch the clock!

This is all well and good, you might say, but what about the possibility of actually getting that type of return? Not to mention the fact that your advisor is telling you that s/he can't guarantee that you will get that return, nor should you risk your capital to seek out a return like that. Well, let me ask you, which would you rather choose? The 1% return like that of a bank savings account, or 12% like that of a more sophisticated investment?

What if you don't stop investing after ten years but keep the same little amount invested over the course of 40 years? How does that look? Well, it's funny, but you actually don't get nearly as big of a bump as you might think by investing an additional $90,000 (30 years X $3,000/yr), but it still is significant.

Return % and Final Value				
Year	1%	3%	6%	12%
1	$3,000	$3,000	$3,000	$3,000
10	$31,387	$34,392	$39,542	$52,646
20	$66,057	$80,611	$110,357	$216,157
30	$104,355	$142,726	$237,175	$723,998
40	$146,659	$226,204	$464,286	$2,301,274

You can see that at 1%, that additional $90,000 only added just over $100,000 over 30 extra years! However, that same $90,000 added over $700,000 at 12%. Which option would you choose? Better yet, how do you get those types of returns consistently?

We'll cover the differences of these types of investments later in the book, but for now you just need to get excited about the possibility of even achieving results like this. I'm getting ahead of myself, but remember, that total return of $1.5 million is from an initial investment of only $30,000! So, how do you get those types of returns, and better yet, how do you avoid paying taxes on a return like that? Well, I'm glad you asked…

What Are Qualified Retirement Plans?

Definition: A qualified retirement plan is a plan that meets requirements of the internal revenue code and as a result, is eligible to receive certain tax benefits.

Qualified retirement plans are what we're talking about in this guide to self-directed investing. Like I mentioned earlier in the book, if your money is in your own bank, checking, or mutual fund account, but the money was not put there through a qualified plan, then it is already considered self-directed. You already have control over your money. So for the purposes of this book we are going to be talking about qualified retirement plan money. What this means is that I am referring to money inside of a defined contribution or a defined benefit plan that you have direct control of, and can therefore choose how it is invested.

So, what are defined contribution and defined benefit plans?

A defined contribution plan is an investment plan most people are familiar with these days. These plans include your IRAs, 401(k)s, SEPs, simple IRAs and so on. These are plans where you "define the contribution" to the plan. Meaning, you say how much you are going to put in and maybe your employer will match how much you put in. As such we are *defining* the contribution. This is in stark contrast to plans of the past.

Defined benefit plans are also known as pension plans. Pension plans, as we'll call them from now on, were created nearly two centuries ago as a way to help people retire, through guaranteed payouts after their working years. These types of plans were actually created to help the economy and help governments to ensure their citizens were not going to die destitute right after they stopped working.

Now of course the defined benefit plans had some great features, but they didn't kick in until around age 65. That's why you always hear about retirement starting at age 65, because that was the age our government decided people would stop working and could start receiving these defined benefit plan payouts.

Of course when these plans were first invented in the late 1800s and early 1900s, people didn't generally live past the age of 65, and therefore the governments generally won. Corporations adopted these models during the second Industrial Revolution in the early 1900s when we started inventing and manufacturing automobiles, rubber, oil, gas, and several different types of industries sprang up. Companies needed ways to entice people off the farms and into their companies. So they started offering defined benefit, or pension plans. This ensured people were going to be able to survive even after they stopped working. These were great plans, however they came with hefty price tags once people started outliving that expected "death" age of sixty-five.

Now that may sound somewhat morbid but let's be honest,

companies are in business to make and keep customers and thereby make a profit. If all of their employees end up living, far and well into retirement and are no longer contributing to the growth and productivity of the company, and thus no longer helping the company to get and keep customers, then they are considered a cost, and as we all know, companies tend to cut unnecessary costs in favor of profits.

As a result these companies ended up spending billions of dollars every single year on their retiree benefits, simply because people were living much longer into retirement than they had originally anticipated.

Therefore, in 1974 when the Employee Retirement Income Security Act (ERISA) came about detailing how defined contribution plans would work, companies jumped on it. These new plans allowed people to contribute, or rather defer their income which meant that people did not have to pay taxes on the money invested that year, and companies were allowed to match a portion of these contributions.

Unfortunately, a loophole permitted companies to switch over entirely to defined contribution plans from defined benefit plans. The government didn't want defined contribution plans to replace defined benefit plans completely. However, the loophole was there nonetheless and smart companies and lawyers figured out a way to get rid of pension plans and the associated costs while still providing some sort of safety net for employees. The problem was that employees did not understand what these defined contribution plans were and as a result many did not contribute to them.

Now most people who are retiring do not have anywhere near enough money to retire and maintain a sufficient standard of living. As a result, society is in this downward tailspin where we're really relying on the government, subsidies, and various other forms of welfare programs to keep a lot of society up and running. I know the reason you are reading this book is because you understand this is a huge problem and is not something that you want to be part of.

As a matter of fact, you likely want to take control of your own situation and be the boss of your own destiny. That is where self-directed investing comes in.

So, I've thrown this term out, *self-directed investing*, several times. Why aren't all qualified retirement plans invested by one's self? Well, the reason is simple- most people don't have the education to invest that money themselves. As such we have what we call fiduciary responsibility that we place in the trust of professionals, financial advisors and planners, and these large investment firms whose sole purpose is to invest your money.

Now that works out really well for these companies. You see, whether the markets go up or the markets go down, these companies are going to continue making money. They do this through fees and various different charges. Their investments are made with your dollars. However, their fees are also paid with your dollars. If the markets go up you make money, but they make a little bit more. If the markets go down, you lose money, but they still make money off of service fees and charges. Unfortunately, many people have no idea how much they are paying for these various fees and charges.

These companies do not have any incentive to let you have control over your money and take it out of their bank accounts, because you're basically taking food out of their children's mouths by doing so. What I mean is if the money is not in their bank accounts to invest for you then they cannot charge you fees for managing and investing your money. As a result they give you a very extensive list of investment options- mostly mutual funds in hopes you will keep your money in their funds indefinitely.

Therefore these companies have a very important role to play in society. People who do not want to learn how to take control of their own investments, do not want to learn how to invest, and want to hand their money over to a professional have these conduits by which to do so. However, you are obviously reading this book because you do not believe this is the right choice for you.

By now you should be piecing together the idea of how the system we have is *slightly* flawed, and most definitely skews in favor of large investment firms on Wall Street and elsewhere around the world. I should know because I've worked for a few of these large firms in the past. However, I'm also hoping that you're getting energized and envisioning what the future will look like for you if you choose to take control rather than give it up. If you're looking forward to learning how to start taking control, then you're in for a nice treat, but first you should know what you are going to take control of, right?

The 401(k)

As I mentioned in the last chapter, ERISA gave companies and governments the opportunity to change the way employees received retirement benefits. Up until this point, a company that was going to offer any sort of retirement benefit only had the option of providing a defined benefit plan. This is where the pensions from General Motors, General Electric, Chrysler, teachers unions, and a whole host of other large organizations really came into vogue. It was a great deal – spend 20 to 30 years working for a company, and then be rewarded with a monthly stipend after you are done working for them. This model worked well for many decades. Unfortunately, the broader economy and demographics played a major role in how this entire environment shifted in favor of companies, the government, and large organizations. Since companies had a higher ratio of workers to retirees during the 1950s and 60s, pension plans continued to amass a fortune of wealth due to the contributions made to their funds through employee deductions and employer deductions.[8] In other words, since less money was being paid out to retirees, more was being held in the coffers of the financial institutions that were housing the funds for these benefit plans. This is what helped fuel the major investment and financial innovations that eventually helped to crash the global economy.

---

[8] Dent, H. S., & Johnson, R. (2011). *The great crash ahead: strategies for a world turned upside down.* New York: Free Press.

Michael Lewis wrote about this back in the 1980's with *Liar's Poker* when he realized how this burgeoning industry was starting to run the show, rather than just remain in the background.

However, as global competition continued to increase, and people began to retire and needed to draw their retirement benefits, it became burdensome for companies to continue to offer defined benefit plans. Is it any wonder then that the government enacted ERISA around the same time these companies were starting to experience more competition from global economies and needed to cut costs? It was at this very juncture that companies began to offer what is now known as the 401(k). The 401(k) is of course derived from the Internal Revenue Code section 401 subsection (k). That is not important to know though. What is important to understand is what happened next.

When companies realized they no longer had to offer defined benefit plans, they immediately switched over and embraced these new defined contribution plans. As I mentioned in the previous chapter, defined contribution plans replaced defined benefit pension plans nearly overnight. Companies did attempt to encourage employees to contribute to their new 401(k) plans, but little effort was given to the financial education and planning for these employees. Instead, human resources departments created nice little spreadsheets and handouts that they could give to new and existing employees that were aimed at helping them understand what a 401(k) plan was and how it could be used to help them benefit in retirement. Of course, most young workers don't really pay attention to retirement planning when they first get out of school or college and get into the workforce. Even worse, senior employees were still expecting and relying on a pension to hold them over in retirement and therefore didn't fully participate in their 401(k) plans. As a result, very few workers were properly investing in their retirement plans in the early years of the new program.

A 401(k) as mentioned earlier is a defined contribution plan whereby an employee contributes a portion of their salary, and an employer may or may not elect to match a certain portion of this contribution. The money is then put into what is called a fiduciary holding account, generally at a large investment company and invested as directed by the employee. The downside of this, apart from employees not contributing enough money to fund their retirement, is that their choices of investments are severely limited.

When I say severely limited I really mean that investments are limited by the asset class. Most investment companies will only allow individuals to invest their 401(k) and other retirement plan money into investments offered by that investment company. For example, you can only invest your Vanguard–held 401(k) into Vanguard investments. These generally take the form of mutual funds, bond funds, and money market accounts. This is all well and good if that's the only way you want to invest your money. However, how many wealthy individuals you know who only own mutual funds or bond funds? The fact of the matter is the mutual funds make up the majority of all retirement plan

63

assets being held at this time, and there doesn't appear to be an end in sight. Take for example the amount of money that has been held in mutual funds over the past several decades. In 1970, there was only about $47.6 billion invested in mutual funds with about 10,700 accounts total. Today, there is _**over \$13 trillion invested in mutual funds**_ with over 264,000 accounts open![9] This is a compound annual increase of 163%! That is staggering statistic by any account.

Getting back on track, a 401(k) is a qualified retirement plan that allows you to defer some or all of your income so that you don't have to pay taxes on that income today. Instead, you end up paying taxes on that income later in life. For many people this is an ideal scenario because most people expect they will be making less money in retirement than they do currently. Therefore, they prefer to reduce the amount of money they are paying in taxes while they're working with the expectation they're going to end up paying less in taxes during their retirement years anyway.

One of the big benefits of investing your money into a 401(k) or similar plan, as opposed to a regular investment account, is the ability to defer your taxes, and thereby lower your current taxable income. There are rules around this process of course. In order for the government to allow you to take such a liberal stance with "their

---

[9] *2013 Investment Company Fact Book*. (2014). Washington DC: Investment Company Institute.

money" they need to ensure you don't have access to your money so it will continue to grow and thus allow the government to collect taxes on your distributions in the future. I say "their money" because you have to realize the government does require us to pay taxes in order to keep up with all the costs of living in the United States. Whether or not you believe in how the government spends our money is correct or not is an argument for another book, so we won't belabor the point here. Instead, what I want you to understand is that the government is giving us an opportunity to reduce the amount of money we pay in taxes currently in hopes we are going to pay more money in taxes later on. In essence the government is kicking the proverbial "tax can" down the road. When the government passed the ERISA laws they were planning to recoup any lost revenues through additional taxes in the future.

What this means for you is that you can essentially reduce your take-home pay today, pay less in taxes now, and increase your investment account all at the same time. Sounds like a great deal right? Well, again there is a catch with this entire set up. The catch comes down to the term "fiduciary". A fiduciary is defined as the following:

Fiduciary: A person legally appointed and authorized to hold assets in trust for another person. The fiduciary manages the assets for the benefit of the other person rather than for his or her own profit.

What this is basically saying is that although it is your money, it must be held by somebody else for the safekeeping and control in order to qualify as a tax-deferred retirement plan. In essence, you are handing over control of your money to another company in hopes that they will have investment options and choices available to you helping you to become wealthy in your retirement years. This is why a lot of employers will not allow you to transfer your existing 401(k) balance to another IRA or 401(k) while you are still employed at the company. Basically, the company has a fiduciary responsibility to you to ensure your money is not spent or wasted since you are relying on this money as a source of income for your future.

Tip: If you are curious to know if you can roll over your money while you are still employed, talk to your Human Resources department and request a "Summary Plan Description". Review the document and look for terminology relating to "In-Service Rollovers". Most companies forbid these for the reasons mentioned above, but some may have wiggle room if you can make a good case.

However, I want you to go back to 2008. Do you remember the term TARP? If you don't, I encourage you to Google it and see exactly what happened to your money when certain fiduciaries were not able to uphold their end of the bargain and keep your money safe for future use. Basically, these large investment banks that were given the responsibility of housing our money and investing in certain assets they thought would be beneficial for your retirement and ended up losing trillions of dollars nearly overnight because they placed faulty bets.[10] The fact of the matter is that these investment bankers were placing bets with your money on investments they did not fully understand and appreciate. They did not understand the entire spectrum of their investments, nor did they appreciate the broader implications of how different sectors of the economy might affect their investment choices.

As a result, millions of people lost significant sums of money while they were invested in assets that they did not fully understand. We blindly accepted the fact that our companies and these investment banks had our best interest at heart simply because they had this fiduciary responsibility to take care of our money and house it until we needed it. Unfortunately, nothing was further from the truth and many of us learned the hard way.

In future chapters I will explain how you can use the benefit of a certain type of 401(k) to invest in assets that you know, like, trust, and understand. Additionally, I will show you exactly how you can take control of your money so that you can invest the way that you want so you can be better protected from any downside in the broader economy than you might have in the past. The fact of the matter is that bubbles and busts are cyclical in nature and are simply a product of capitalism at work. When you turn your money over to someone else and expect

---

[10] Roubini, N., & Mihm, S. (2010). *Crisis economics: A crash course in the future of finance*. New York, N.Y: Penguin Press.

them to take control of your money and act in your best interest, you are simply fooling yourself and setting yourself up for failure. As you learn more about these different types of retirement plans, you'll come to understand and appreciate the value that having true control of your money.

In the next chapter we will dive into how anyone, even people without a 401(k), can really benefit from proper retirement planning.

Individual Retirement Arrangements

An individual retirement arrangement, or account as it otherwise known, is simply another type of qualified retirement plan that allows an investor to put money away tax-deferred so they can invest in assets without having to worry about incurring taxes on their investments or allow their investments to grow tax-free altogether.[11] There are many different types of individual retirement accounts, but the most popular one is the traditional retirement account or traditional IRA. A traditional IRA works somewhat similar to a 401(k) in that a person can invest their pretax money into a qualified retirement plan thereby reducing their overall tax rates in the given year.

Individual retirement accounts can also be used to invest in different types of assets. However the main difference between an IRA and a 401(k) is where the money is housed. A 401(k) is housed with a fiduciary, also known as a trustee, whereas an IRA is held with a custodian. Both the trustee and the custodian act in the same manner in most cases. These are generally institutions that are regulated by the Financial Industry Regulatory Authority (FINRA) and the Securities and Exchange Commission (SEC). They provide investment options such as stocks, bonds, mutual funds, and other publicly traded

---

11 Internal Revenue Service (2014). Individual Retirement Arrangements (IRAs). Retrieved from http://www.irs.gov/Retirement-Plans/Individual-Retirement-Arrangements-(IRAs)-1

securities.

It should be noted at this point that there are several different types of investment options available to individuals. If you simply look at the world around you, you will see investment opportunities everywhere. From the printer that made the book that you are reading right now, to the Kindle that you might be reading it on or the iPad you used to search Google to find this book, or if you are like me, the glasses you need to read something like this. All of these different inventions were created by some sort of company; they came from some individual with an idea, were placed into action through a research, development, and manufacturing process. The raw materials were then sourced from somewhere within the world, transported to the right facilities, shipped overseas, assembled by laborers or machines most likely, and eventually delivered to a retail store where you bought it. Just within the process of getting you the format to read this book were several dozen different types of investment opportunities. Many involved businesses that may be found on a publicly traded stock exchange such as the New York Stock Exchange (NYSE), but many others may not be listed on any public exchange. I don't want to belabor the point here, as we will devote an entire chapter to investment options available to you, but I do want you to be aware that there are options out there other than just investing in stocks, bonds, and mutual funds.

The main difference between a 401(k) and IRA is the fact that an IRA is not sponsored by an employer. You do need earned income (but not too much), but otherwise almost anyone can have an IRA. This is one of the main reasons that the IRA came into existence. People needed a way to invest their money in some sort of qualified plan outside of their employer's plan simply because many employers did not offer a defined contribution plan such as a 401(k) when the IRA was introduced. In fact, when Gerald Ford signed the Employee Retirement Income Security Act in 1974 (ERISA), there wasn't very much thought given to the fact that corporations may begin to adopt this practice of laying the burden of retirement on employees instead of shouldering the burden themselves. In doing my research, I wasn't able to determine that the purpose of ERISA was to remove the burden of retirement from businesses altogether. Instead, the idea was that individuals would be given another way of saving for retirement and helping them overall, but not completely eliminating pension plans.

One point that needs to be understood is that the government wanted to introduce retirement plans as a way for Americans to begin saving for their own retirement because they did see danger on the horizon as individuals were not saving enough money to fund their own retirement. There was speculation as to whether or not Social Security was going to be able to provide a sufficient standard of living for retired individuals back in the 1960s and '70s. Obviously today that idea is still very real and even scarier. As a way for Americans to be incentivized to put money away for retirement, the government offered tax-deferred retirement plans like we're discussing here. I bring this point up again because it is vitally important to what I'm about to discuss with regards to contribution limits.

Contribution limits are placed on all types of retirement plans simply because the government does not want people to put every dollar they earn into these types of plans and therefore not pay any income taxes. Let's be honest, the government may be full of fools sometimes but when it comes to ways to get at your money, they have that part figured out pretty well. As a result, the government imposes strict contribution limits or maximums on the amount of money that can be contributed to an individual's retirement account every year. When it comes to IRAs, contribution limits are much lower than they are for 401(k)s. In 2014 for example the maximum contribution to an IRA is $6500 whereas that investment can be up to $23,000 for a 401(k).[12] The main reason that 401(k) contribution limits are so much higher is because lobbyist groups from the business sectors, and business owners themselves, wanted to find ways to write off even more of their income against taxes when the laws were presented. Since many congressmen and congresswomen are also business owners, I'm sure they wanted to find a way to reduce their overall tax burden as well.

---

[12] Internal Revenue Service (2014). *Retirement Topics - IRA Contribution Limits*. Retrieved from http://www.irs.gov/Retirement-Plans/Plan-Participant,-Employee/Retirement-Topics-IRA-Contribution-Limits

This is important to understand because later on when we talk about self-directed retirement plans you'll want to have an idea as to why I suggest one over the other. Now, everyone's situation is different and you should definitely consult your own financial advisor whenever it comes to planning for your own retirement, but I will lay out very compelling reasons for choosing one type of account over another in certain circumstances.

Roth or Traditional?

In the two previous sections I've mentioned that your money can be contributed to a retirement plan in either a tax-deferred or tax free situation. However, what exactly does this mean?

In 1997 Bill Clinton passed the Taxpayer Relief Act which permanently placed into effect the Roth provision for retirement plans. Sen. William Roth of Delaware was the chief legislative sponsor who helped to create this provision in the rule.[13] The Roth provision allows investors to contribute money to the retirement plans with after–tax dollars. In essence, the earned income you receive from a job has already been taxed at your current tax rates, and what is left is allowed to be contributed to your Roth plan and allowed to grow tax-free. However, the money that you contribute to a Roth plan is not deductible in the current year and cannot be used to reduce your current taxable income.

By contrast, many people still have a traditional form of retirement plan that allows them to deduct their contributions in the current year thus reducing their overall taxable income in the year in which they make the contribution. This can prove quite useful for individuals who are already in a high tax bracket and would like to figure out ways to

---

[13] Roth IRA. (2014, October 16). Retrieved October 17, 2014, from http://en.wikipedia.org/wiki/Roth_IRA

reduce their current taxes. However, the main drawback of a traditional style retirement plan is that your distributions you take from your plan during retirement are then taxed at your current tax rates.

The dilemma most individuals face is whether they should attempt to reduce their taxes now in hopes they will be in a lower tax bracket in the future, or take the hit now and not have to worry about paying taxes on their distributions later. There have been several articles written on the cost-benefit of using a traditional versus a Roth retirement plan and unfortunately the results are inconclusive. This stems from a wide array of issues relating to the premise for retirement planning and investing in general. Almost every single scholar who attempts to perform a cost-benefit analysis of retirement plan contributions and distributions assumes that individuals will only make a modest return on their investment and further assumes they will not be making a greater income when they retire.

Another stumbling block for individuals who contribute to a traditional plan is the required minimum distribution imposed by the government at 70 ½ years old. In other words, after you retire the government ensures that they are going to get some of their money back by forcing you to take distributions from your retirement plan even if you don't need. As a result, if you invested in a traditional retirement plan you will be forced once again to pay taxes on your distributions once you reach 70 ½ years old.

It is impossible to look into the future and see what our future tax rates will be. However given our current economic situation and out of control debt, it is very likely that our tax rates will increase in the future in order to keep up the pace of paying down our debt and maintaining our standard of living in the country. For this reason, many advisors will suggest you choose a Roth style retirement plan. However, if you are currently in the highest tax brackets then you may want to consider using a traditional retirement plan in order to reduce your current tax rate. Each individual's situation will be different and this is where having a professional on your team to help with understanding the tax rules and codes will be instrumental in proper retirement planning.

If you are a very savvy investor and feel that you can get an incredible rate of return on your investments inside your retirement plan, then it may be wise to choose a Roth retirement plan so that you can grow your investments tax-free and therefore not have to pay any taxes on your capital gains in the future. If you don't think that you are going to be able to reap massive returns on your investments (which means you aren't implementing the investment strategies listed the end of this book), then you may wish to use a traditional retirement plan and reduce your taxes now. Again this assumes that you will be in a lower tax bracket in the future, which is very difficult to ascertain.

You should also be aware that several employers are now offering a Roth provision to their 401(k) plans which allows you to contribute both pretax and after-tax dollars to your retirement plan. This is definitely an area in which you should investigate a little further because it may make sense to invest both types of monies into this plan. The reason is that if you can reduce your taxable income, pay less tax, and still have enough money left over to invest that it may make sense to utilize both features in the same plan. The big drawback of these types of plans is that you will be required to keep very accurate records of what money is pretax and what is post tax. This is of course one of the benefits of having a large investment institution handle your money- they take care of all the accounting issues.

Just realize that whatever type of plan you choose, whether an IRA or 401(k), you do have the ability to put money in to either a traditional or a Roth style plan. The Roth provision for 401(k) plans (as well as 403(b) and 457(b) government plans), but it does require that the plan administrator adopt the rules for the Roth provision in order for you to be able to take advantage of this tax-free investment solution. I personally know several individuals who are getting five and six-figure checks into their Roth investment plans completely tax-free of capital gains which of course boost their retirement significantly.

Insurance

One of the most important aspects of planning for retirement is being properly protected in the event something unfortunate happens to you or your family. After all, what good is it to amass a wealth of material possessions, money, and assets if one accident can reverse all of your fortune and send your entire estate into complete disarray, or worse, into somebody else's hand? I have personally been helping people understand insurance and risk management for over 10 years and I've had to explain the reasons for insurance time and time again. No matter how many times I tell people about insurance, or how many different ways I frame it, people still don't fully understand the need for insurance and the purpose behind having insurance. In many companies, this lack of understanding on the part of the consumer is what helps agents to procure a new client. Believe it or not, many people are still either uninsured or under insured and this bodes well for life insurance representatives who can paint a very dire picture of doom and gloom should anything happen to you or your loved ones. As result, people will sign up for life insurance before they have any sort of game plan on how to increase their wealth at the same time. The fact of the matter is that you do need insurance. There are several different types of insurance which insure against casualties, loss, and other mishaps that could set you back several thousand dollars and several years of planning. However, one of the major misnomers about insurance is that you should get insurance first to ensure against every possible casualty out there without paying attention to how much it is going to cost. To me, it makes sense to build your wealth while at the same time remain *properly* protected as your wealth grows. The "properly protected" piece is where a good financial planner can help you.

A good financial planner will help you to understand insurance and the various types of insurance before they ever try to sell you a policy. Additionally, a good planner will sit down with you almost every year if not more frequently to identify any gaps in your coverage and to ensure that you're properly covered in all aspects of your life. As we grow and mature, buy homes, have children, acquire assets and so forth, our insurance needs change. Any financial planner who is worth their fees will make sure you sit down with them on a regular basis to review your insurance policy and ensure your policies are keeping up with your changing lifestyle. As an example, look at the table below showing two hypothetical cases of two individuals at different times in their lives. You can see that when Mary is younger and single, doesn't have any kids, and doesn't have a mortgage, her needs for life insurance and other types of insurance is very minimal compared to when she has children, a husband, a home, and various other assets in her name. If Mary were to purchase the policy when she was 20 years old because the rates were great but didn't increase her coverage over time, she is likely under-insured should anything bad happen to her, her family, or her possessions.

Potential Risks for Mary	26, Single, no Kids	46, Married with Kids
Vehicle?	Yes	Yes- multiple?
House?	No	Likely
Children's education?	No	Yes
Personal Assets (furniture, jewelry, etc.)?	Minimal	Several Items
Disability needs?	Minimal	High
Medical Needs?	Minimal	High
Income requirements?	Low	High

After you get done with this chapter you will understand insurance just enough to be dangerous! I'm not going to write an entire book on insurance as there are several hundred books out there that can help explain it in much greater detail. However, I want you to understand where insurance plays into your retirement plan so that you understand what type of policies you should be acquiring and make sure that you are properly covered every step of the way on your path to wealth and freedom. So, what are the types of insurance you should have at various stages throughout your life? The types of insurance available to you are as follows:

- Life insurance (permanent or temporary)
- Health insurance
- Long-term care
- Property and casualty
- Liability
- Homeowners
- Renters

- Auto
- Umbrella liability policies

- Business
- Malpractice
- Equipment breakdown
- Cyber crime
- Identity theft
- Employer's liability
- Accidental death and dismemberment
- Gap insurance

Obviously not all of these insurance policies will be needed by every individual. However, most will be applicable for you at some point in your life. Many policies may never be needed or economically viable for you, though it doesn't hurt to check.

Let's take gap insurance for example. Gap insurance is generally required if you finance a brand new vehicle. In the event your vehicle is totaled in an accident, a bank making the loan to you on your vehicle will need to be sure that the loan will be paid off in spite of the fact that you no longer own the car. If you purchased the vehicle brand new, then you will most likely owe more on the loan than the car is worth shortly after purchasing the car. A car insurance policy will only pay for the actual replacement cost of the car, and if that is less than the loan on the vehicle, you will be stuck with the difference. That is gap insurance.

Equipment breakdown, malpractice, and business insurance coverage is likely only going to be needed by business owners or high net worth individuals who have vast estates. These policies are very specific to the needs of the individuals or companies purchasing them, but for sole practitioners or business owners, it's very important to understand what they are.

Umbrella coverage and liability insurance are absolute musts for people with a reasonable net worth or valuable assets not covered under other policies. Imagine having one of your kid's friends over one day and they decide to play on the swing set and slide out back, which happens to tip over and injure your child's friend, God forbid. If the child is injured severely or the child's parent just wants to get some money out of you because they know they can, you better have a good homeowner's liability and/or umbrella policy in place to help out. This is true for auto insurance as well.

Insurance is a way to help "make you whole" after an accident or unfortunate event. For that reason it is important to have proper coverage for your situation. Victims of Hurricane Sandy still remain without a home or compensation because they didn't have flood or wind insurance on their property, and they didn't know! For that reason, you need a good insurance agent or advisor on your team.

It's smart to have a good team in place before a disaster strikes. However, the game is sometimes rigged against you. What happens when the game you are playing isn't the same as the officials in charge? That is the topic of our next chapter.

How the System Is Broken

I previously mentioned how in the early 1970s there were little over 10,000 mutual fund accounts open in the entire country, and how that number has ballooned by over 2400%. As with almost any new trend, many people join the bandwagon very early on and experience surprising gains and returns before everyone in the entire marketplace catches on. Then, as a trend begins to pick up a little bit of momentum, more and more people start to join the circus lifting asset price to ever higher heights. Eventually the frenzy will stop, and before you know it the bottom has fallen out and only those smart enough to get out on the upswing made any money. This is a trend we've seen in the stock market (and of course mutual funds) over the past several decades. When these were new investment vehicles many people rushed into them because they understood that they could start to spread their money across different types of companies. This of course of what became known as diversification and everybody drank the Kool-Aid.

At about the same time, baby boomers for the first time ever became stewards of their own finances and investments. Not knowing anything about how to invest or what to look for in the markets, they relied on financial advisors who were peddling these new forms of investments known as mutual funds. Everyone believe the basic premise that if you diversify across multiple companies you will eventually be safe enough to where you won't experience any loss on your investments. Now of course every prospectus and every investment ever sold to the public during this time had a little disclaimer at the bottom that said "*past performance is not indicative of future returns*". Very few people actually thought about that during the frenzy where we rode the stock market up. However, since that verbiage and other such wording let financial firms and investment advisors off the hook, they couldn't be held accountable for selling bad products, or worse yet, not understand the products they were selling to begin with.

It is an unfortunate fact that many financial planners don't truly understand the investments they are selling to their clients. In fact even the Securities and Exchange Commission (SEC) exams are geared more toward understanding rules and laws as opposed understanding the underlying principles of valuing investments. Granted, there are many courses that teach investment valuation and investment strategy, but not all advisors take these courses and are therefore ignorant in many areas with regards to what they should be selling and how they should be selling it to potential investors. Robert Kiyosaki quips "They are called brokers because they are *broker* than you!" Now to some extent he is correct in that many financial advisors start with nothing, get their series 6 and 63 licenses, and then work for a company selling mutual funds with very little training on how to read markets or financial statements.

As a matter of fact I myself was on that track originally but decided

I wanted to understand investing more than I want to understand rules and laws in the beginning. So I poured myself into investment education materials rather than learning about the Securities and Exchange Commission rules so that I would have a leg to stand on when I needed it. It was after I learned how to value an investment and a company that I began learning the rules and laws surrounding selling securities to the public. My goal is to create value and pass the information along to others so that they can make informed decision for themselves, not just act as a mutual fund sales representative

I digress. You can start to see how the current system we have for retirement planning may not be correct simply because the people who are being looked to as advisors are not fully aware and understanding of the psychology of the market, nor how best to plan investments for *your* future. Investing is actually quite a complex game if you intend to invest only in publicly traded stocks. The fact of the matter is that you have imperfect information on which to base the value of the company, and you are also competing with investors in the billions if not trillions of dollar ranges. Even Warren Buffett needs the power of Berkshire Hathaway to invest at his level. However, that is the majority of what financial advisors and planners are selling: publicly traded stocks.

In order for investment companies to profit, they must charge fees from each of their clients in order to ensure their continued prosperity. These fees have all sorts of different terms- load, transaction, assets under management, etc. Each of these fees is taken directly from the investor whether or not the underlying investments increase in value. In fact, the SEC actually has rules in place to ensure that financial advisors and registered investment advisors cannot participate in the profits of an underlying investment with their clients.[14] This of course limits the ways in which some of these companies can make money, so it only makes sense that they would pass these expenses of running investment agencies to the clients, right?

However, it was only a couple years ago when the government finally decided that these fees must be disclosed to clients since they were overwhelmingly opaque and difficult to ascertain in any case.[15] It is not clear yet whether or not companies are going to reduce the fees that they charge their account holders or if they'll just find different ways to obtain these fees, much as banks did when they could no longer profit from their own investments.

There are two types of fees that are charged for a 401(k) at most

---

[14] United States Code. (2012, January 3). *15 U.S.C. 80B-5 - INVESTMENT ADVISORY CONTRACTS*. Retrieved 2014, from US Government Printing Office: http://www.gpo.gov/fdsys/granule/USCODE-2011-title15/USCODE-2011-title15-chap2D-subchapII-sec80b-5

[15] United States Code. (2012, January 3). *15 U.S.C. 80B-5 - INVESTMENT ADVISORY CONTRACTS*. Retrieved 2014, from US Government Printing Office: http://www.gpo.gov/fdsys/granule/USCODE-2011-title15/USCODE-2011-title15-chap2D-subchapII-sec80b-5

companies:

Expense Ratio Fees: This ratio incorporates the administrative, investment management, and marketing fees charged to savers. Because these fees do not vary much from year to year, they are reported as a static expense ratio and listed both in a retirement plan's summary documents and the individual prospectuses of each mutual fund in the plan.

Trading Fees: The costs incurred by a mutual fund when buying and selling the securities (bonds, stocks, etc.) that comprise the fund's underlying assets. Investment managers of mutual funds pay a fee each time they buy or sell one of the securities that comprise the underlying assets of the fund, and they pass these on to savers via the funds' share prices. Trading fees vary from year to year depending on the frequency with which fund managers buy and sell the funds' assets.

All in all, these fees can add up to about 3% of a given return. So, if your fund averages a 7% annual return, and you pay 3% in fees, you end up with a net 4% annual return. Not so awesome, is it? Basically, your 7% annual return quoted in the prospectus can be cut by nearly 1/3 due to excessive fees!

If you do the math, and I don't want to bog you down with the details, the average dual income household making an average salary each year and contributing to their 401(k) religiously could lose as much as **$153,794** due to fees and lost returns![16] For some people this can be the equivalent of a few years worth of their salary lost simply to pay for the benefit of having retirement plan to begin with.

One thing is clear though: financial planning and investment agencies make the majority of their money off fees they charge their clients. Many of these companies rake in billions of dollars in profit every single year from these fees, which in and of itself is not necessarily a bad thing wouldn't you agree? The part that I take issue with is when these companies continue to rake in billions of dollars every year even though the markets plummet and investors tend to lose the majority of their money. In fact, in spite of inciting one of the greatest financial crises since the Great Depression bankers and Wall Street executives alike raked in billions of dollars in bonuses alone in 2009 when the financial crisis was at an all-time high. To add insult to injury, these bonuses were paid with tax dollars that you and I used to help bail out some of these financial firms that caused this crisis. Again, I don't take issue with having to bail out these firms in order to keep our economy afloat, but I do take issue with these bailouts not trickling down to the consumer who needs the help the most and instead lining the pockets of the executives who are most responsible for this crisis.

Are you beginning to see how the current system is rigged against

---

[16] Hiltonsmith, R. (2010). *The Retirement Savings Drain.* New York: Demos.

you? In many cases you are given investment options that are not suitable for your investment criteria, and on top of that you are being charged out the rear for these investments. Not only are you being charged for all of these different expenses in your retirement plans and investment accounts, but you are also not being given a good opportunity for proper investment selection. True, there are over 8500 different types of mutual funds out there, and several thousand publicly traded stocks and companies, but what are you really being offered?

The fact of the matter is that there are more mutual funds out there than there are publicly traded stocks. Just think about that for one second. A mutual fund is a conglomeration of different publicly traded stocks generally organized around some sort of criteria such as valuation, sector, geography, or any other number of selection criteria. The goal of course is to diversify your investment portfolio to protect against risk. However, if there are more mutual funds than stocks then doesn't it just make sense that most of the stocks will end up being in multiple mutual funds? In fact that's very true. A stock in a large capitalization value fund, or in other words the stock of a very large company, could also be lumped in with a healthcare sector stock fund. This means that if you happen to own shares in both of these funds the new risk is truly not diversified because you own the same stocks in multiple funds. Therefore, if the value of that stock goes down then the value of the associated fund will also go down in relation to that stock's decline. Now of course the theory is that if the entire healthcare sector goes down, not all large-cap stocks will go down as well. In that sense you are somewhat diversified and should, *should* being the operative word, be protected from the downward slide overall.

Unfortunately, even if you choose all the correct mutual funds for your investment portfolio one fact still remains – all of your investments are tied up in the stock market. Since there are several different types of investments out there, we don't want you to "diversify" within just one asset class, but rather diversify across several sectors of the economy. In part four of this book I will talk more about the different investment options available to you, and we'll talk about different case studies you can read to learn more about how you can invest in these different asset classes. For now, you just need to know that investing in the stock market alone is not the best plan of action.

Another big issue with current 401(k) plans is how they incentivize employees to invest in the current company for which they work. Humor me as I go through a story with you about my own personal past. After getting out of the Navy, I went to work for a company called Hartford Steam Boiler. This company specializes in providing equipment breakdown insurance coverage for large companies and focuses on providing inspection services for these companies in order to reduce its overall risk. However, the company was owned by a larger insurance company, American Insurance General, otherwise known as AIG. Now you can probably read the writing on the wall but let me continue. One of the incentives of AIG was to provide employees with a discounted stock price if they purchased AIG shares through an employee stock ownership program, or ESOP. This stock ownership program gave employees a sweet deal. If at any point during the year you purchased AIG stock, you got a 15% break on the lowest value of the stock that year. I know many individuals personally who invested in this employee stock ownership program, but for one reason or another I didn't. Perhaps I was lucky because at the time my wife and I were just starting out and I didn't have enough money to continue to invest into a company I worked for.

Now, fast forward a few years and I remember going into the office one day to do some training and there on the pegboard in the office was AIG's share price of $62. At this point I was thinking it might be a good idea to start investing a little bit more into the company and maybe even starting to put more money away in my 401(k) plan. I started off by putting money in my 401(k) and maximizing my investment there so I could reduce the amount I paid in taxes each year, as well as start to build a nest egg for my family.

Just as I was beginning to look into the employee stock ownership program more, the shit hit the fan with AIG. Without going into too much detail, AIG began insuring mortgage-backed securities and when the housing market slumped significantly, many of these securities became defunct. AIG was on the hook for paying the insurance policies on these mortgage-backed securities. Unfortunately, the company didn't have anywhere near enough money to cover all of its losses and as a result was insolvent. When investors saw this they panicked. Just a very short while later, I remember going into the office again and seeing AIG share price down at around $3! Shortly thereafter, AIG had to create a 20 to 1 reverse split of its stock just so it could remain listed on the publicly traded stock exchange. In essence, if you held 20 shares of AIG before this catastrophe, you now only held one!

This catastrophe was unthinkable by so many people in the financial world, let alone average employees who didn't know much about investing in the financial markets. Unfortunately, so many people had invested in this employee stock ownership program and were almost wiped out completely. I personally know of a couple individuals who had to extend the retirement simply because they lost so much money when AIG went under.

This again highlights the pitfalls of investing in just stocks, and even investing in a company that you think you understand, as I did. I was lucky in the sense that I was either too ignorant or too broke to invest in my own company, but many others were not. This again is another lesson on diversification. However, hopefully you are beginning to understand that diversification in the sense that most financial planners are telling you is not true diversification, and that you need to have a broader understanding of investment options available to you in order to mitigate the risks of down markets.

Okay, perhaps you are now beginning to think and realize that you need to be in a safer alternative because the stock market may not be your best solution, right? What are your alternatives then? Are you going to run to your bank and put your money into a certificate of deposit or CD? Maybe you'll start to put your money into bonds? Unfortunately, all of these different assets are actually one and the same to a certain extent. They are all considered paper assets. When you invest in a bond, CD, or stock, you are basically hoping for appreciation on that investment, which is a derivative of the piece of paper you signed and received for your investment. In other words, if the company whose stock you bought fails to appreciate in value, or the value of the stock goes down, then you can either sell at a loss or wait and hope that the stock goes back up, or you can recoup your money through dividend payments. If you buy a bond for the same company, then you are basically guaranteed to receive your money before the stock purchaser receives any if the company goes bankrupt. However, don't be fooled into thinking that all bondholders are always paid. The recent financial crisis and European debt crisis are shining examples of how bond payers can be wiped out as well.

The above examples are your typical investment options when you are looking at your 401(k) retirement plan investments currently. However, there is a better way. The whole purpose of this book is to open your eyes to a new way of investing, one that we call Self-directed Investing. I'm going to talk at length about self-directed investing in

95

the next part of this book and I hope you are taking notes because there's a lot of information to cover.

A Personal Note

I want to make sure that I make something perfectly clear about the financial planning industry and several of its practitioners. I do not believe that financial planners are bad people. In fact, I have been a planner and an educator for a very long time, and am lumped in with the rest of the financial planning industry, so I don't want people to think of the entire industry as a sham.

In all honesty, most financial planners I have met are some of the most honest, loyal, and caring individuals one could hope to know. In several respects they are the exact type of people you would like to have on your team. However that doesn't mean they are necessarily the best qualified individuals to help *you* achieve *your* financial goals. Most financial planners do believe that the investments they are selling are of sound quality and rival that of any other firm in the industry. However, the fact remains that they continue to offer investment instruments that may not necessarily be conducive to your long-term goals.

If on the other hand you have found a financial advisor or planner who has recommended that you diversify across several asset classes and not have all of your money in their company's portfolios, then you have probably found a very good advisor. In essence, financial planners and advisors always strive to do the right thing by their clients, but are generally hampered by the constraints of their licenses and the companies they work for. Wall Street has managed to create a sprawling empire of investment firms focusing on their own bottom line, not yours. This is why it is important that you continue to read books like this one so that you can get the best education and be properly prepared when you work with your team of financial advisors and planners.

Part 2
A Different Approach

What is Self-Directed Investing?

In order to understand self-directed investing, one must first have a frame of reference for what investing is in general. When I say self-directed investing, what I generally refer to is investing in a retirement plan of some sort. The reason these plans are called qualified plans is because the IRS qualifies them to certain and special tax treatments and tax deferral, allowing the end user to participate fully in a plan that will lower their current tax bracket or their future taxable income.

We use the term self-directed investing only to stipulate qualified retirement plan investing simply because investing out of your savings account or checking account is already considered self-directed investing, primarily because the funds are already your own. In order to understand what I mean by your own, I'm going to lead in with a story.

My great-grandmother was born in the year 1900. She survived the Great Depression, she had hardly any money to her name throughout most of her life. Her husband ended up losing a leg due to disease and illness. He ended up dying very young and she ended up living most of her adult life as a single mother.

My great-grandmother was a teacher, originally in Chicago then eventually in California during these lean years. She knew exactly what it was like to get a paycheck, walk down to the bank, deposit the money in the bank, and then have the bank close just a few short hours later. Can you imagine having a young child at home, a disabled husband and all of a sudden finding out that your entire month's paycheck just disappeared like that, in the blink of an eye?

As a matter of fact it's true. It happened to her, it happened to millions of people during the Great Depression era and it's happened to millions of people since then believe it or not.

However, I don't want to lament on all the past historical problems right now. Instead what I want to tell you about is what my great-grandmother did for me, personally. You see, she somehow managed to recover from that horrible tragedy, where she was left almost penniless with a young child at home and a disabled husband. She managed to pick herself up by her bootstraps, so to speak, and eventually ended up retiring very well and very successfully as a school teacher, a very admirable career no doubt.

Now mind you, my great-grandmother lived during a time when there was not a social safety net, so to speak. There wasn't social security when she began working and therefore she understood that she was required to provide for herself or her family had to provide for her, at the time of her retirement. Of course back then this was a common concept and everyone understood that. However, in the 1930s and 1940s eventually people began to rely more on the government for these types of living arrangements post retirement because we realized that the financial burden of retirees on the economy was so great that it required some sort of safety net in place to prevent total collapse.

Now my great-grandmother lived to 103 years old, far surpassing most life expectancy tables at the time. Of course this also meant she lived well into her retirement years and was going to need some sort of assistance. She did of course have help from her daughter, my grandmother, as well as other family members. She also did something amazing in spite of needing assistance in her retirement years. She managed to save enough money for her great-grandchildren to actually have some of their own investments in order for us to go to school.

Now I personally joined the Navy when I was 18 years old, so I didn't really require any money for a college at the time. Instead, my great-grandmother decided to pass the money on to me for my safe keeping, use, and benefit, which was incredibly generous of her. The sum total of her gift to me equaled approximately $20,000. I thought this was an incredible gift, one that I cherished and hold very dear and close to my heart to this day.

The money I received was invested at Oppenheimer at the time. I'm sure you've heard of them? Well when I went to the financial planner who my great-grandmother and grandmother had been working with, I was told I couldn't do very much with *MY* money. I could buy certain types of life insurance policies, I could invest in various mutual funds, but I was told that the money was stuck inside these accounts.

I didn't fully understand that at the time, nor did I really appreciate what the financial advisor was telling me. Furthermore I didn't do my own research. Therefore I was left young and naïve, with a lump sum of cash I'd never had before, which was already invested for me. In talking with my financial advisor, what he told me was, and I quote, "The technology sector is booming right now, and since you are young I strongly encourage you to invest in it."

Now, young, impressionable, wide eyed and bushy tailed so–to–speak, I was very naïve and really wanted to believe this individual had my best intentions at heart. So I went along with his recommendation and invested in the technology sector. I was also a technocrat and to this day still. I really do appreciate technology and learned to love technology and embrace the changes that have come with technology.

What I decided to do was invest in a fund primarily centered on mid-cap growth stocks in the technology sector. I didn't understand any of what that meant at the time. All I was told was that it was a new fund, and the managers were exceptionally bright. Everyone expected this sector to go off like and do very well by me and everyone else invested in the fund.

Remember, this was the late 1990s and anyone who lived through that era, the "dot-bomb" as we call it, knows full well what happened after that. You see, what ended up happening was the money my great-grandmother had spent decades accumulating and preserving for me,

104

disappeared almost overnight. I was devastated. I was frustrated. I was angry. I was mad at my financial advisor. I was mad at myself for not doing anymore research. Basically all the money I had in that fund was gone. This is something that has stayed with me to this day and has led me down my current path.

Now that fund is still available and if you look at the chart over the years you will see that shortly after I invested in the fund, it devalued significantly (from a high of $8.05 on December 31, 2001 to a low of $3.99 nine months later). As a matter of fact, my little nest egg dropped by a factor of 50%! Fifty percent when you have most of your eggs in one basket is quite a hefty sum. As a side note, I would recommend that you do not have all of your eggs in any one basket, at any time.

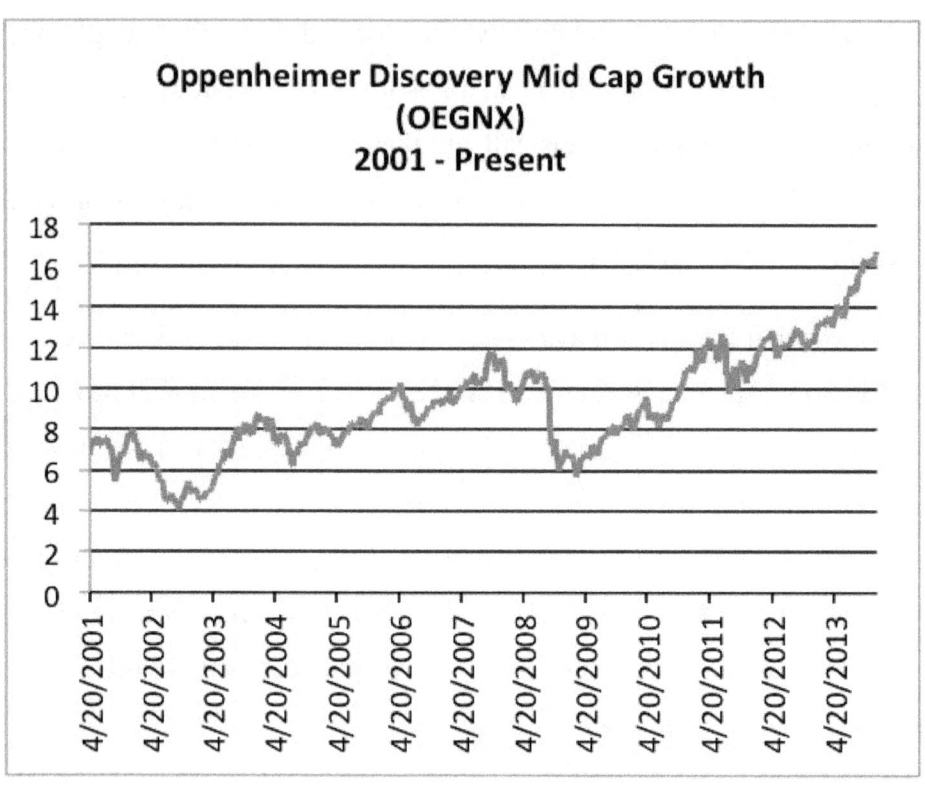

Oppenheimer Discovery Mid Cap Growth (OEGNX) 2001 - Present

I decided to do what any frustrated investor would do. I took my money out. Now of course every financial advisor would tell you that you're supposed to stay in it for the long haul, weather the ups and downs, and eventually your money will come back, right?

Again, I was young. I wanted the money for various other things. I wanted to be able to pay off some debts. I wanted to be able to buy a car, and I did of course want to pursue my college education. So I decided to take the money out, albeit at a substantial loss.

Now you might be thinking, "Well that's just ridiculous! I don't know why you would want to do that? Why would you even think of doing that?"

You also have to remember what the economic situation was at the time. The mood was similar following the financial crisis. Many individuals thought the technology boom was never going to come back; that it was a bust gone forever and most of our money was just never going to come back.

As a matter of fact the NASDAQ rose to over 5,000 points during this time. Nearly tripling what its previous high had been. In 1996 the NASDAQ was around 1,000 points. By 2000, when I was looking at this fund, the NASDAQ had crested 5,000! Shortly thereafter, by around the middle of 2002, it had fallen back down to below 2,000.

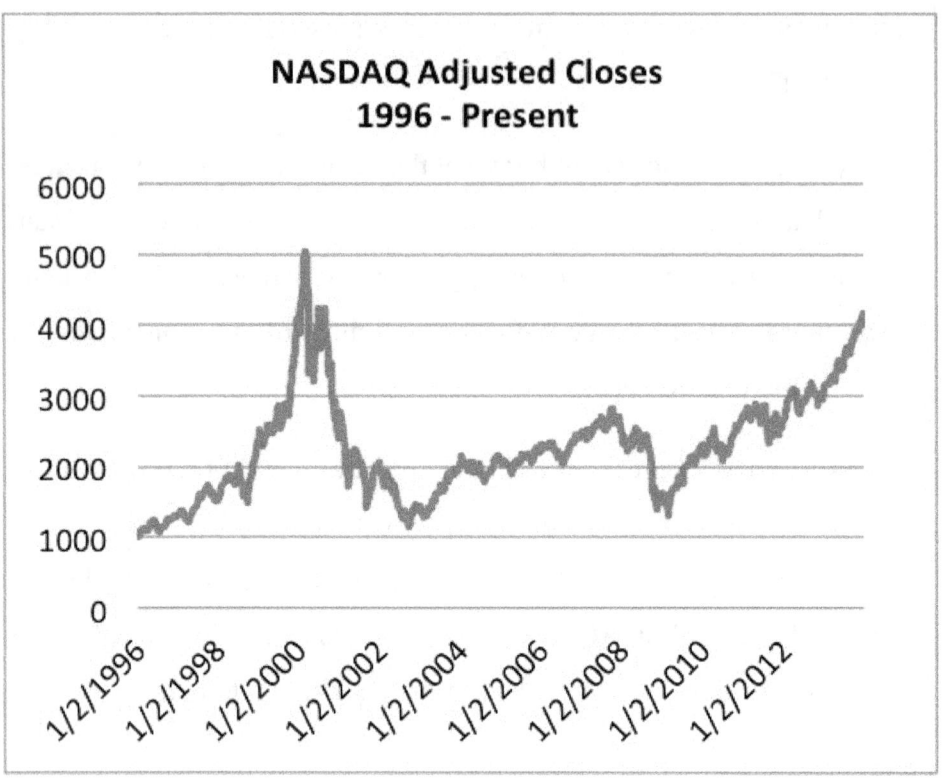

**NASDAQ Adjusted Closes
1996 - Present**

Since the NASDAQ was composed primarily of technology stocks, people who invested in this sector lost heavily and also didn't think it was going to rebound anytime soon. We thought the internet was just going to be a bust. No one believed in it. Investors on Wall Street were pulling their money out in droves, which continued to drive the market down even further and as a result people lost billions of dollars in a matter of a few short months. Trillions of dollars were lost throughout this dot-bomb.

So, getting back to my story, as a result of this loss I decided to pull my money out and invest in other things. I decided to pay off some loans. I decided to pay off some debt. I decided to get a vehicle, a reliable one, so I wouldn't have to keep working on my car. I did a lot of things that may have been childish and silly at the time. However, I didn't see the market coming back and I didn't see me ever getting the money back that I lost.

Fast forward to today, almost fourteen years later. That fund has averaged an annualized return of about 5%. Of course, there have been ups and downs and the majority of this 5% gain has occurred in the last couple of years. For nearly ten years, after I had lost that money, this fund had not done anything. Hadn't gone up, hadn't gone down, and if I'd weathered it for ten years I wouldn't have been much better off, especially if you take into account inflation and the fees I was paying on the account.

I may have received a few dividends here and there but not much to speak of. Just in the last three years this fund has performed pretty well. But if you average it out over the last fourteen years, it's averaged about a 5% return, nothing to write home about.

Let me put this into perspective for you. Let's say I went and did some retirement planning on my own, and I'll show you this in a little bit, and I determined that I needed $1 Million, in order to retire at the age of 65. If I started with the $20,000 my great-grandmother gifted me shortly before she passed away, and kept getting a 5% annualized return, and not putting any other money into this fund, it would take me approximately 80 years to reach that $1 Million mark. Eighty years at 5%! This is an exceptionally long period of time, and of course when you're eighteen years old, 80 years seems like an eternity.

So I wasn't about to sit in and let my money accumulate at 5% per year. Now of course, you might be saying, well of course Jeff, but you would be adding money to this over those years as well, so it would end up being a lot shorter. True. If the market continued to go up at 5% per year and I was able to put money in, it may have been shorter. But we all know that markets go up and markets go down.

We'll talk about another story in a future chapter about a person who tried to time the market for their retirement and what exactly happened to them. But I understood enough at that young age to know that markets go up and down, and without having direct control of my investments and understanding my investment criteria, I was never going to be able to retire at this rate.

Self-Directed Investment Plans

There are primarily two different types of self-directed investment plans. One is an IRA or individual retirement account. As mentioned previously, these plans were brought about because the government wanted individuals to be able to invest money outside of their employer sponsored plans and still be able to have some sort of tax incentive to save money for the future.

Now remember the government gives people incentives to put money into these types of plans as a way to ensure there isn't a drain on the economy down the road when people are no longer able to work and produce sufficient income to cover the costs of living. The incentive provided, as mentioned earlier, is a reduction in income taxes owed during the year in which an individual makes contributions to their plan. Allowing you to defer a portion of your income today so you have an income later in life is one way for the government to ensure they continue to have tax revenues when individuals retire.

However individual retirement accounts have limitations. One of these limitations is a phase-out of the ability to contribute to the plan if you make too much money. If you have a substantial income then contributing to an IRA is completely out of the question. This doesn't mean you can't have the plan at all; you just can't contribute any tax-deductible money to the plan. Unfortunately this means you need some other sort of qualified plan if you are in a high income tax bracket and want to reduce your taxes.

Another issue with IRAs is that you have a very low ceiling for how much you can contribute. At the time of this writing, people are allowed to contribute $5,500, unless you are over the age of 50, in which case it jumps up to a whopping $6,500 per year. Now, if you're making $100,000 per year, dropping your income down by $5500 a year so that you can reduce your taxable income isn't really going to have a major impact is it? Additionally if you're only able to put in $5,500 per year into an investment plan, you're not going to have a substantial base by which to invest your money and grow your investments for some time.

As you can see in the table below, there are phase-out limits for IRAs that don't pertain to 401k plans. For example, if you earn $200,000 from your job, then you simply can't contribute to your IRA plan. However, that same individual can still contribute up to $23,000 to a 401k plan. Note that the $260,000 income limit is simply the limit for calculating contributions, not a limit on whether or not you *can* contribute.

Additional rules apply IRA contributions that do not affect 401k type plans. One such limit imposed is on the ability to contribute to an IRA if you are offered an opportunity to contribute to an employer-sponsored plan. If you are covered by a workplace retirement plan, then the phase-out limit for an IRA drops from $178,000 down to $95,000. In essence, the IRS is limiting the total amount of money you can defer on an annual basis, thereby lowering your taxes.

Type of Plan	IRA	401k
Contribution Limit	$5,500	$17,500
Catch Up Limit	$6,500	$23,000
Phase-out Begins (married)	$178,000	NA
Maximum Income Limit	$188,000	$260,000
Phase-out Begins (single)	$112,000	NA
Maximum Income Limit	$127,000	$260,000

IRAs are really good for several reasons. There are several very good investment options you can choose with an IRA, and we will cover these investment options in the next section. But for some people these options just aren't good enough.

Now if you don't have any investment or retirement plan, I strongly encourage you to get some sort of IRA post haste! Whether it's a Roth or traditional IRA at this time, it does not matter. However, we do not know if or when the tax codes might change, or if these types of plans will be offered in the future at all. There are some really great benefits to having an IRA and hopefully being grandfathered in should tax codes change. So do yourself a favor and get an IRA of some kind if you don't already have one. Doing so could mean the difference between living a comfortable retirement or needing help after a lifetime of hard work.

The other type of self-directed retirement plan is what's called a Solo 401(k) or individual 401(k). A Solo 401(k) plan is just that: an individual 401(k) plan for a single person or married couple. Now the reason these can be self-directed is because they bypass a rule within the IRS covering full time employees. However, the stipulation is that the individual who wants a Solo 401(k) must have or be starting a business of some sort. This is where a 401(k) differs greatly from an IRA. Barring any income thresholds almost anyone can have an IRA- as long as you earned income, you can contribute to an IRA. However, only business owners and self-employed people or couples can get a 401(k). Don't worry, if you're not self-employed yet, we will talk about how you can still get into this amazing type of plan later!

Solo 401(k)s are limited to businesses that don't have full time employees. Companies with any full time employees cannot have a "Solo" 401(k), but rather a standard 401(k) such as what you might have with your current or former employer.

So what are the requirements to having a Solo 401(k)? Well, quite simply, you must have some sort of business, which you can set up now or in the future, that has a reasonable expectation of making money.

Now, what does that really mean? That really means you can have your own individual 401(k) at any time, set it up, fund it with other retirement plan money through a rollover, and then start the business operations after the fact. It's not a requirement to have your business up and running and *making money* before you set up your 401(k). The only major requirement for a 401(k) is that you have no full time employees in the business that adopts the 401(k) plan.

There are a number of differences between a 401(k) and an IRA, as I outlined above. Two of the major differences between these two types of plans come down to contribution limits and control. With an IRA we already talked about the contribution limit being a maximum of $6,500 at the time of this writing. A 401(k) has a maximum contribution limit of $52,000 with a catch up of another $5500 for those over 50 years old. If you are married, you and your spouse can work in the business and double your total contribution to $104,000! Even if you and your spouse both contributed to an IRA and you were both over 50 years old, the maximum you can contribute as a couple is $13,000. So as you can see there is a huge difference between contributing to a 401(k) versus an IRA.

I suggest you go to:

www.AngelNetwork.com/innercircle to get access to additional resources that outline how exactly you can contribute the total amount to a 401(k) plan and take full advantage of these types of tax deductible contributions.

The other main difference between these plans is control. Both of these plans can be self-directed, meaning you can have a self-directed allowing you to invest in many different types of investment options including alternative investments. However with an IRA you are required to have a custodian who holds and monitors your money. In order to invest your funds from a self-directed IRA, you must send the custodian a *direction of investment* letter stating how you want to invest your money. The custodian then writes the check to whomever or whatever institution you are investing in or with. There are still guidelines on what you can and cannot invest in with custodians, and they have very strict rules on how to go about processing these directions of investment. If you don't do anything with your funds in a self-directed IRA, the money just sits in the custodian's bank account collecting a paltry interest rate on your money. You can see how using an IRA, although more structured, can also result in delays and headaches with investing your money.

As an example, if you attempt to invest in something the custodian doesn't understand or finds confusing, you are required to furnish even more documentation to prove it is a legitimate investment. This means that it can take a significant amount of time to complete and process your transaction. Additionally, there can be fees involved with each direction of investment letter you create.

With a 401(k) you have what is called checkbook control. With a 401(k) you have a trust account, with a trustee who is in charge of the money. The beauty of this setup is that the **trust is yours** and **you can be your own trustee!** This means that if you have an investment option that comes along, and you are the sole person responsible for making the decision to invest, you can also be the person who writes the check for the investment.

Now of course you are still required to have clear documentation on the investment, and you must also have a reasonable expectation of that investment producing money in order for it to be considered a qualified investment. However, done properly this gives you direct access and control of your money, whereas with an IRA your money is housed in another account under the purview of a custodian where you have little direct control.

Those are the two primary differences between an IRA and a 401(k). Take a look at the chart below to see even more examples of the differences between these types of accounts.

	IRA	401(k)
Contribution Limits (of individual)	$5500 ($6500 for 50+)	$17,500 ($23,000 for 50+)
Company Matching Limit	$0	25% of Profit, up to $34,500
Can Be Self-directed?	Yes	Yes
Can Invest in Alternatives?	Yes	Yes
Tax Deferred?	Yes	Yes
Tax Free Withdrawals?	Yes	Yes
Employer Matching?	No	Yes
Checkbook Control?	No*	Yes
Subject to Unrelated Business Income Tax?	Yes	No
Easy to set up?	Yes (through a custodian)	No (unless you have a company who specializes in them)
Roth Provision?	Yes	Yes

The IRA LLC

If you have been doing your own research up to this point, then you may very well have heard of a term called the IRA LLC. An IRA LLC is a limited liability company that is wholly owned by the funds in your IRA. In other words, you went out and created your own limited liability company and have the sole member as the IRA who then proceeded to invest in the newly formed company to capitalize it.

The benefit of an IRA LLC is that you now have a company that is able to perform the duties needed to invest in a qualified investment. You, as the owner of the IRA, are now allowed to act as the manager of the LLC thus being the sole person who can make a decision determining the efficacy of an investment. This eliminates the need for a custodian and a direction of investment to the custodian to make the underlying investment.

However, as you will see in a case study in this book, having an IRA LLC does not necessarily guarantee complete flexibility of your investment. There are still rules and limitations on what can and cannot invest in with your IRA LLC as well as how the proceeds can be distributed once investment has paid off. For example, you cannot fund the IRA LLC with qualified money (that which is from your IRA) and also with your own nonqualified money (that which is not in your IRA). Doing so would violate some of the self-dealing rules we will talk about later and could thus trigger a tax, penalty, and invalidate your entire

IRA.

Additionally, if your LLC is responsible for making payments to any entity surrounding the investment you have chosen, then you cannot personally use your money to pay the LLC's bills. This again would violate the self-dealing laws in place. Your LLC also not pay you a salary as that again would result in a prohibited transaction and self-dealing.

Having an IRA LLC may sound like the best of both worlds for many individuals. After all it does include the use of a custodian who is generally very adept at handling qualified retirement plans. It also provides you the opportunity to have direct checkbook control so that you can make an investment with how going back through your custodian for permission and access to your money. However, the drawbacks of having an IRA LLC are numerous, and could result in inadvertently violating some of the self-dealing and prohibited transaction rules.

One such drawback is that you now have a limited liability company that is required to maintain its own documents and records separate from the IRA, and may have to pay its own formation fees and taxes in various jurisdictions. In some states having an LLC can cost upwards of $1000 per year to keep the business in operation. For that reason be sure to check with your advisors to ensure that using an IRA LLC is the best option for you. Another drawback can be that you are now running a company but you cannot take a salary or any sort of payment from the company at any time. Remember, businesses have operating agreements, financial statements, accounting, payroll, and other activities that can make it very burdensome on the owner if they are not familiar with the requirements.

The benefit of having an IRA LLC is that you do maintain your IRA status, but have direct access to the money in the LLCs operating bank account. This means that if an investment does come along you are able to write a check from the LLC to cover the cost of the investment. Any returns on that investment that come across as prophets of the LLC will flow back directly into your IRA tax-free or tax-deferred, depending on whether you have a Roth or traditional setup. Just be sure if you do set up an IRA LLC that you do not run afoul of the IRS rules and regulations we will discuss in the next part of this book.

Why a 401(k)?

I've now talked a lot about the different types of self-directed retirement plans, but which one is right for you? Quite honestly, only you can answer that question. It's important to understand what your goal is when choosing a plan. And hopefully after the last section you understand the difference between the two available self-directed retirement plan options.

Some questions might help you decide if having a self-directed plan is even right for you in the first place:

- Are you going to be investing in mutual funds? If so, why bother? You can use a non-self directed plan to invest in mutual funds with your current custodian most likely.
- Will you be investing in the stock market?
- Do you want to invest in foreign exchange?
- Are you going to be investing in real estate?
- What about gold, silver, oil, gas, etc.?
- What does your overall retirement plan look like?
- Are you seeking to invest for cash flow or appreciation?
- How much money are you going to need before you can actually retire and live off the income return?
- How much time do you have before you retire?

All of these questions and many more need to be answered before

123

you can make the right retirement plan selection for yourself. One of the biggest advantages of having a retirement plan to begin with is the tax advantage of saving and investing. When I talk about tax-advantaged savings, what I'm referring to is the amount of money you could put away every year that will help to reduce or eliminate your personal or business income tax. As I mentioned previously, contributions for each of these types of retirement plans are limited, but the 401(k) plan offers a much higher ceiling of up to $57,500 per year. This is a substantial savings in your taxable income every year simply by choosing the right retirement plan.

Of course in order to take full advantage of this $57,500 contribution limit, you must be self-employed, over 50 years old, and have no full-time employees. This does of course weed out the great majority of individuals out there, but for the few who do want to run their own business and ensure they have a way to minimize their taxes and save for retirement at the same time, this is an incredible option not available to most. Now if you don't have your own business, or you already have full time employees, this doesn't mean that you can't utilize the benefits of a 401(k) anyways. It just means that your contribution limit may be limited to $23,000 as an employee. However, if you are self-employed or have your own business you can still put a stipulation inside your own 401(k) plan to match contributions up to a certain amount for all employees. This is similar to what most Fortune 500 companies do already, but their matching contributions are

124

generally very limited.

Another great benefit of having a 401(k), whether you are self-employed or still currently employed at another company, is the ability to take out a loan against your retirement plan. This option is limited to 401(k), 403(b), and 457 Government plans and is not allowed in IRA plans. The rules and regulations surrounding loans from each of these types of plans are different and can vary from plan to plan. However, to make things simple let's say you have a 401(k) plan with $100,000 currently vested (vested just means the money is yours). In the case of a 401(k) plan, you are able to withdraw up to 50% of your plan balance, or $50,000, whichever is less. There really aren't any limitations on what you can use the proceeds from your loan for. However, there is a very strict requirement that you pay back the loan into your own 401(k) account.

This is a very important point, so please be sure to reread the section if you need to. Your loan can be used for various purposes such as funding education, repairs on your home, starting a business, or even buying your own home. However, in each of these situations you are required to pay back the loan directly into your 401(k) account with interest. The beautiful thing about this type of loan is that you are paying yourself back with interest. Instead of having to take out a loan from a bank and pay the bank money, you will receive the benefit on both ends of the loan, both the receiving and repayment side.

In most cases, you will have a maximum of five years to repay the loan balance. The one exception to this is when using the money to finance either the whole price or a down payment on your own personal residence. In this case you are provided up to 15 years to repay the balance of the loan.

I want to make it very clear that using a 401(k) loan, or a loan from any of your retirement plans should be considered a last resort for the purposes of getting money. There are many other options available to most individuals out there that do not require tapping into future retirement funds. The reason I make this disclaimer is because many individuals wrongly assume that once they take the money out of their 401(k) plan that they are allowed to do whatever they want with it and not worry about any possible consequences. As a result, they fail to make timely repayment of their balance and end up running afoul of the rules imposed on these types of loans. If you fail make a payment the IRS can deem that your entire loan was instead a distribution subject to early withdrawal penalties and taxes. If the whole purpose of getting a loan was to avoid paying taxes and fines, then this is the last thing you want to do.

Another strategy that many promoters are advocating these days for 401(k) plans is what is called the "Roll Over Business Startup" strategy. Basically this strategy allows an individual to roll over the entire balance of their 401(k) plan into an individual 401(k) plan, and then start up a corporation that adopts the 401(k) plan. The money from this

401(k) plan can then be used to purchase stock of the Corporation thus capitalizing the newly formed business. I strongly encourage you to avoid this strategy for several reasons. The first and main reason to avoid this strategy is because you should not be putting your entire retirement account balance at risk to start a new business. After all, the business success rate in our country for new businesses is approximately 5%. This means that the majority of people starting a new business have a 95% chance of losing all of the money they put into their new business. If you were to do this and lost your entire retirement portfolio by making poor business choices, then what is the likelihood you would be able to recover?

I'm not suggesting that you are a bad business person or wouldn't be successful, but I am suggesting again that putting all of your eggs in one basket, especially an unproven basket, is not a wise financial decision. Going back to the beginning of this book, the purpose of having a retirement plan in place is to ensure you have a steady stream of income when you no longer can or desire to work. If you put all of your retirement plan at risk before this day comes and end up losing all of your money, then that stream of income you are hoping for has vanished along with any chance of an enjoyable retirement.

As you can see, there are several benefits to having a 401(k) plan, the least of which are the tax benefits for contributing to the plan. You already know that you can grow your money tax-free or tax-deferred in a retirement plan, but of course what you really want to do is grow that money faster and have more control over how the money is invested. The next chapter is going to show you how you can begin to identify investment options that are suitable for your situation and retirement plan goals.

Self-Directed Investment Options

We've talked a lot about different types of plans and what self-directed investing is, but I haven't even explained why self-directed investing is important. Sure, I've mentioned control, right? But why do you need control of your money?

I gave you a story previously about how my money would have taken 80 years to grow to a point where I could actually retire, at which point I will probably be long gone, and that doesn't work for me.

What is the true purpose of taking control of your money? Well the primary reason is to be able to retire when you want, how you want, where you want, and have an income stream that will support you for as long as you need. That's not to say that a normal non-self-directed retirement plan won't get you where you need to go. In fact it is very possible that you could choose the right financial advisor and the right financial plan in order to get the return on investment you need to properly secure your retirement. You could do this using a mutual fund, bond fund, or various stocks that are offered by a broker or their company, and you may very well be able to retire when you want, how you want, and have the income you want.

However, most financial advisors work for large investment companies and are told to sell certain types of investments. These investments generally come in the form of mutual funds. As I noted earlier, there are more mutual funds on the market today than there are stocks on stock exchanges. This is akin to having more All-Star teams than there are baseball teams in the Major League. It doesn't necessarily make sense, does it?

One of the major downsides of investing primarily in mutual funds and stocks is that you are relying on appreciation as your main source of wealth creation. The problem with appreciation to grow your wealth is that it involves several factors outside of our control. Market forces and economics play a significant part in the overall appreciation of the stock market. Anyone who remembers Black Monday or the Flash Crash can tell you that appreciation can be a fickle beast not to be tampered with! During each of these situations, market forces beyond any one individual's control drove stock prices down through the floor in a matter of days, or minutes in the event of the flash crash. This of course takes its toll on people aiming for stock market appreciation to secure their portfolio positions.

Everyone will tell you to never try and time the market. I don't know of any financial advisor or planner who has ever said you should try to time the market. But let's be honest, that's what you are doing in the case of appreciation. You are investing in one class of investment, one asset class, and you are relying on appreciation to help fund your retirement. When you rely on appreciation you are hoping that everything is going to continue to rise so you will be able to fund your retirement lifestyle.

If we take a look at the tech boom of the late 1990s and early 2000s, let's see how this appreciation strategy plays out. Let's say I was an individual who had $1 million stored up in my retirement plan in 1999. Then let's say I had the majority of my money in the Nasdaq. Below you can see how the value of my shares in the Nasdaq composite index changed from 1999 to a peak in 2000, then a trough down into 2003. Notice how the value changed by a huge factor over that time? What if I was planning to retire in 2003 and didn't take my money out in 2000 because everyone thought the tide would keep rising? My $2 Million portfolio plummeted to only about $500,000! Remember, this isn't just one stock or sector, it's an entire market!

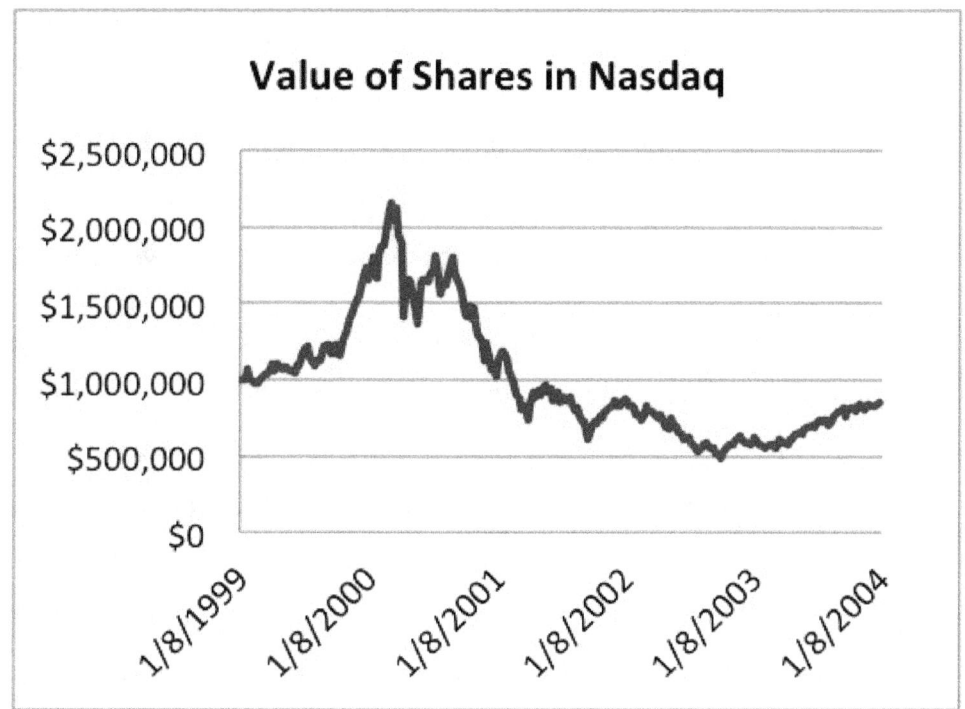

Let's assume for argument sake that I was 60 years old in 1999 and was ready to retire at 65 years old in 2004. As you can see from the previous graph, my $1 Million nest egg in 1999 ballooned up to over $2 million in just a couple of years. Like most people, I was getting a bit greedy and was waiting for the value to climb higher and higher. However, in 2000 and 2001 the value started dropping and I started getting worried. However, everyone says to invest for the long haul and stay the course, so I did. By 2003 I was losing my mind and devastated to see my portfolio crash around $500,000, only half of the value a few years earlier!

So what do I end up doing? I end up working even longer than I wanted. I end up delaying my retirement. As a matter of fact, this is what millions of Americans did during this recent financial crisis in 2008 and 2009. People had to put their retirement plans on hold for an average of five to ten additional years in order to be able to survive their retirement years and maintain the quality of life they wanted.

Going back to my situation, I am now 65 years old, not enjoying the thought of working longer, but know that I can't keep my current lifestyle without a steady paycheck. So, foolish me, I decide to leave my money invested in an asset class that is geared for appreciation, not income, and is also prone to terrible cycles. I figure that I'm almost back up to my $1 Million mark, so let's just leave it in place a little longer. Now, you can see by the graph below that everything is starting to rebound, so I'm getting excited again. My goal is $1.2 Million to retire, so I'll just hang on until then.

Unfortunately, we all know what happens before I get to my $1.2 Million goal, right? The housing crisis hits and the financial markets begin a rapid meltdown. By February of 2009, when I'm 70 years old, my portfolio has dropped again to less than $600,000, again only half of what I need to retire comfortably. Now I'm forced to rely on Social Security and might be lucky to have a pension, but I'm not traveling around the world like I planned, nor am I spending lavishly on my retirement because I fear for the future and my health.

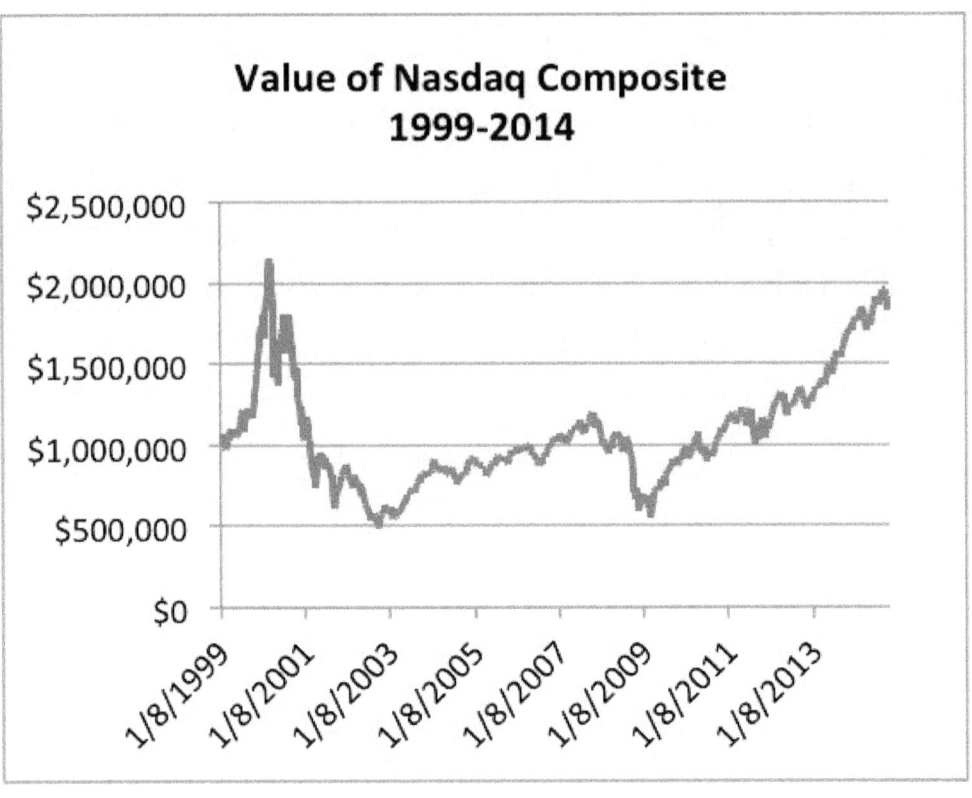

Value of Nasdaq Composite 1999-2014

For some individuals this has been a sobering reality; their health has deteriorated and they can no longer work. As a result they are forced to live in a less than ideal situation because they can't afford their previous lifestyle.

The biggest problem with investing using the traditional mindset of buy and hold investing, is that you are relying on appreciation which is a very dangerous game to play. Even investing in fixed-income securities wouldn't have helped my situation too much because many of these went out the window during the financial crisis and some even lost value due to negative interest rates! Regardless of what your belief is about asset allocation, the truth remains that relying on appreciation is a risky proposition at best!

Alternatively, self-directed investing gives you a choice. It gives you the option to take control of your money and invest in a way that makes sense to you. When I say invest in a way that makes sense to you, that may not mean anything to you at this time. However, with proper education and guidance you will fully understand and appreciate what control of your money can do for you.

There are several different options for investments out there. Many of which are not touted by financial planners who work for large financial firms. As I've alluded to previously, this is because their licenses and compensation structures don't allow or encourage investing into alternative investments. Further, many people aren't experts in these areas, and therefore decide to forgo advising on them altogether rather than seek out a competent partner to help.

Here is a list of investment options available to you at any time, whether in a self-directed investment account or just in your own individual bank account. We are going to cover some of these asset classes in much greater detail in later chapters.

- Stock
- Bonds

- Mutual funds
- Life insurance it or not though, the IRS does
- Real estate
- Private businesses
- Oil and gas exploration
- Alternative energy
- Foreign exchanges
- Currencies
- Commodities such as oil, silver, gold etc.
- Collectibles (art, gold coins, etc.)

Note that collectibles are actually prohibited investments per the internal revenue code for a qualified retirement plan. Examples of collectibles are coins, stamps, books, works of art, and other unique items that can be good investments for knowledgeable buyers. These types of investments require some sort of specialized knowledge in that industry or sector, but are not really considered investment options according to the IRS.

Okay, so knowing these different types of investment options is imperative to understanding how you can actually direct your investments for better returns, better income security, and overall better financial health and wellbeing. The choice is yours. But you need to know that you have choices before you even begin down that road.

I will cover more about investment options and choices in part four, but before we get to those investment options I need to cover the *danger zone* of self-directed investing first.

Part 3

The Danger Zone

Unqualified Investments

Believe it or not there are actually investments that are not allowed to be used inside your retirement plans. I very briefly mentioned that collectibles such as art, coins, etc., are actually not allowed to be held inside your retirement plan. There are several other investment options that are not allowed to be held inside your retirement plan for various purposes. I'm going to list each one of these down separately so you can have a full understanding of why you cannot invest in each of these asset classes, and if possible, a way that you could invest in some sort of derivative of these asset classes if you choose.

Collectibles

This is the first and easiest one to identify because it's explicitly called out in the Internal Revenue Code.[17] In fact, the IRS specifically states which types of collectibles they deem unworthy to be inside an IRA or other retirement plan. I've listed these that are called out by the IRS specifically below, and underlined additional investments that I have added that we've also found to be illegal for the purposes of investing inside your retirement plan:

- Artwork
- Rugs
- Antiques
- Metals - with exceptions for certain kinds of bullion
- Gems
- Stamps
- Automobiles
- Coins
- Alcoholic beverages
- Certain other tangible personal property
- Baseball Cards
- Furniture
- Silverware
- Toys
- Comic Books

Believe it or not though, the IRS does actually make exceptions for certain types of coins. This is a somewhat gray area, and since I am not a subject matter expert on coins themselves, I will just give you the

---

[17] Internal Revenue Code. (2013) *Publication 590 (2013) individual Retirement Arrangements*.

basic reason why some coins are allowed and others are not. The material reason for allowing certain types of coins to be collected inside a retirement plan is simply because the precious metal content of the coin itself is deemed to be more valuable than the collection of coins. In other words, if your coin is pure gold, and you decided to melt the gold for other purposes such as bullion to be sold on the market, then the investment could be allowed. However, this is still a gray area and unless you are an expert with investing in coins, I strongly suggest you seek out the advice of a professional before you decide to try and buy coins inside your retirement plan.

On that note, the IRS also mentions that metals are not allowed to be held inside retirement plans, but I just talked about gold being allowed...what gives? Well, as you can see in the bulleted list above, it does mention that certain types of bullions are allowed. In fact, gold bullion is allowed to be invested inside of an IRA, but not inside of a 401(k).[18]

---

[18] Swisher, P. (2014). 401(K) INVESTMENTS: Stupid investment tricks: Interesting, risky, or downright dumb retirement plan investments. *Journal of Pension Benefits, 21*(3), 33-37.

Derivative Positions

Now again, I am not a subject matter expert on derivative positions such as naked call writing, or even covered calls. However, I do know what is and is not allowed inside of your retirement plan. To give you some basic information, a "naked call" is "An options strategy in which an investor writes (sells) call options on the open market without owning the underlying security."[19] In essence, what you are permitting here is an unlimited risk inside of a retirement plan. Without in-depth knowledge of these types of transactions, it is very difficult to determine what type of risk you are actually exposing your plan to. As I mentioned in an earlier section of the book, the whole purpose of a retirement plan is to mitigate risks for you as the beneficiary of the plan so you can live a long and fulfilling life with income security. By permitting your plan to have an unlimited risk potential, you are violating the basic tenet of risk management and mitigation inside of your retirement plan portfolio.

---

[19] Naked Call Definition | Investopedia. (2012, January 1). *Investopedia*. Retrieved January 6, 2014, from http://www.investopedia.com/terms/n/nakedcall.asp

Life Insurance

In general, no type of life insurance can be purchased in your retirement plan. This includes permanent and temporary types of insurance. In other words, you can't have your retirement plan be the beneficiary of a life insurance policy and receive a payout in the event the insured passes away. There is an exception to this, known as the *incidental benefit rule* which allows the plan to receive a small (i.e. incidental) benefit should a plan participant pass away. In general, I would steer clear of this type of investment anyways as it does cause some consternation for the IRS and requires detailed calculations to be performed if life insurance is purchased in the plan.

One way that a plan could potentially invest in life insurance policies is through the process of investing in a *Life Settlement* investment. These types of funds are set up to purchase life insurance policies on aging or terminally ill individuals who would prefer to have their cash now rather than just pass the benefit onto the beneficiaries. For example, someone who has Stage 4 lung cancer and has a $1 Million policy in place may want $300,000 to pay for treatment or just make their last few months more enjoyable and comfortable. A life settlement option allows individuals to give the person a portion of the policy payout in exchange for being named a beneficiary. This can be a win-win for everyone, but there are a lot of challenges to investing in these assets properly.

If you are interested in learning more about how you might be able to benefit from investing in Life Settlements, go to www.AngelNetwork.com/InnerCircle for more information.

The basic premise for retirement plan investing is that you want income producing assets that will spin off cash flow and possibly appreciation. This is a very general rule, and of course there are exceptions. However, if you keep this notion in mind, you are less likely to purchase an illegal investment that could derail your retirement.

Self-Dealing

One of the things we have not covered is why self-directed investing is not so prevalent throughout our financial system already. One of the main reasons that self-directed investing is not ubiquitous is simply because of all the rules governing retirement plans and investing in general. Since self-directed investing is a relatively new concept in the world of investing, there is a lot of gray area when it comes to precedents. Precedents dictate a lot about how we operate in many legal fashions. What this means is that various courts have ruled on certain cases that have come before them in the past and set standards and guidelines for how we operate. Since self-directed investing is a relatively new area, there isn't much legal precedent for much of what has been covered. This shouldn't scare you though, because there is actually some precedent since certain people have violated the rules of the Internal Revenue Code or Securities and Exchange Commission (SEC). This chapter is going to deal with how you can avoid becoming one of these court cases and setting a new precedent for future self-directed investors.

One topic that is very difficult for many people to understand is what is referred to as self-dealing. Since retirement plans are designed to only be withdrawn from once the beneficiary has reached a certain age, 59 ½ years old at this point, there are a lot of rules around how the money can be invested and accessed prior to that age being reached.

This is the main reason we have retirement plans to begin with. The government has decided we need to put away a certain amount of money for the time when we cannot work and provide our own income, which is why they allow tax-sheltered investments in the first place. The money is meant to be set aside and not touched or taken out until such time that we can no longer work, or at least no longer want to work, so we have an income once we stop producing goods and services through a job. For these reasons, the government has very strict regulations about what you can and cannot do with your retirement plan money while it is invested and you are not yet at retirement age. In order to prevent people from taking money out or benefiting from the retirement plan money, there are rules that prevent an individual from dealing directly with their own money. This is known as "self-dealing". In other words, if I have $100,000 sitting in a retirement plan at anytime, I can't use that money to go out and buy a car, a house, or any other personal item that would benefit me directly, unless I do so through the 401(k) participant loan mentioned previously. The money is meant to be invested into a qualified investment so I can earn a return for my future retirement. This is really important to understand because there are several ways that an individual can engage in self dealing without even realizing it. For example, let's say I buy a second home thinking that I'm going to rent it out the majority of year. Well if that home is in Hawaii and I've decided that I want to go to Hawaii for vacation I can't actually stay in that vacation home simply because my retirement plan purchased the property. This would be considered self-dealing.

Another way someone could perform a prohibited transaction through self-dealing is by paying themselves a salary out of a company they formed using their retirement plan money, as in the case of an IRA LLC mentioned in an earlier chapter. A recent court case outlines how an individual purchased a car dealership with their retirement plan money (yes, it is legal) but then decided to pay himself a salary out of the car dealership's income so that he could pay his own personal bills (Terry L Ellis and Sheila K Ellis, Petitioners V. Commissioner of Internal Revenue, Respondent, 2013). This is of course frowned upon by the IRS and is considered self-dealing. As result, the investors (husband and wife) ended up having to pay taxes on all of the income produced by the company, as well as an early withdrawal penalty because they were under the age of 59 ½. See the case study at the end of the chapter for additional information

Again, this is a very important point to note because it outlines simple little ways in which an investor can go awry of the retirement plan rules and regulations. It's important to understand that your retirement plan must be completely separate from you, and you must not accept the money inside your own retirement plan at any time for purposes other than investing or distributions in accordance with the plan rules. Self-dealing occurs in many different types of transactions. We've already discussed how using a rental home for a vacation home is completely illegal, as well as paying yourself a salary out of a company that your IRA or 401(k) account owns. But are there other ways you could inadvertently engage in self-dealing without being aware of it?

The fact of the matter is that yes, in fact you can engage in self-dealing without even knowing it. Let's say for example that you decided to purchase a rental property through your retirement plan because you wanted to use real estate as an investment option. Of course this investment option is completely legal as we discussed in the previous chapter. However, the property requires repairs, and to get a renter to pay the maximum rent you have decided to rehabilitate the property. Since you want to save money on the property, and enjoy working on projects like this, you decided to do many of the repairs yourself.

The very act of performing work on a rental property, regardless of whether or not your retirement plan owns it, is considered an activity in which you are "actively engaged" in the work on the property. Since the whole purpose of having retirement plan is to have a passive investment portfolio, engaging in active investment pursuits or active management of the investment is considered self-dealing. In this case, even though you didn't put any money of your own into the property purchase but rather just did the work on your own, you still actively participated in the investment which would be considered a self-dealing transaction and could result in severe penalties, fines, early distributions, taxes, and lawsuits.

150

So why would anyone want to have a self-directed retirement plan to begin with if there are so many ways an individual could result in losing their entire retirement plan? It's a good question, but as you learn more about how you can invest passively and reap better rewards and returns than you could in other traditional investment options, you will see that there are several different ways to make more money faster by utilizing self-directed investment options. Take for example an individual who had several hundred thousand dollars in his retirement plan. This individual was barely keeping up with inflation by having his money in a money market fund and savings account. Instead, he simply wanted to beat inflation and keep up with the rising cost of living. After all, he was retired and did not want to actively pursue any investments on his own. However, he was very hot on the idea of investing in real estate, but he didn't have the wherewithal, the knowledge, or the desire to actively fix, flip, rehab, or rent out the property. Instead, we showed him how he could take his money and lend it out to various real estate investors and developers who are in the field of real estate and whose area of expertise was real estate.

Basically the same type of transaction was occurring as in the previous example: a property was purchased; it was then rehabilitated and brought to market; the property was then rented out for long-term gain. The big difference however, was that our client only used the money in his retirement plan as a loan on the property, and was able to receive payments from the investors who took the time to fix up the property and rent it out. This investor had absolutely no dealing with anybody who was performing the work, marketing the property, or renting it out. Instead, he simply put up his money as a passive investor and collected loan payments while his money was being used by the real estate investor.

Another way to do this is by partnering with an investor who wants to do the same type of transaction, instead of lending money to the investor. In this case, the retirement plan and the interested third-party investor form an LLC to purchase the property; the retirement plan money is used to fund the LLC and has an ownership interest as a limited partner. Now, the important thing to note here is that the IRA or 401(k) is not the managing member or operator of the LLC. Instead it is simply just a passive investor that owns membership units in the LLC. Now, the LLC Company goes out and purchases the property, performs the necessary repairs, and eventually sells it for profit. The investor then gets the deposit back into his retirement plan after the transaction has closed and the profits have been realized.

In this example, the profits could be one dollar, or it could be $1 million. It doesn't matter. All that matters is that the IRA or 401(k) was a passive investing partner, or a silent partner in the deal. The returns could either be considered tax-free if it was a Roth account, or tax-deferred if it was a traditional retirement plan account. In either case, there were no capital gains taxes paid on the investment simply because it was owned by the IRA or 401(k).

So, now you can see why it is important to go about investing in your retirement plan through the proper channels using the right kinds of tools and advice so you don't end up in a self-dealing or prohibited transaction situation. Prohibited transactions can result in massive penalties of 150% of the account value, as well as taxes, fines, and lawsuits that you would end up paying for if you ended up violating the rules of the IRS. In our next section we are going to talk more about prohibited transaction and how you can avoid them altogether or at least spot a potentially prohibited transaction so you know what to avoid before you get into it. Self-dealing is one of the major concerns of the IRS and they are targeting it very aggressively these days simply because there have been so many different court cases coming out of the woodworks as a result of these new types of self-directed investment plans. Below is one such example.

Self-Dealing Nightmare

In March 2011, the Ellis' received a very unpleasant surprise from the Internal Revenue Service. To their dismay, they received a bill in the mail that they were not expecting. A bill that totaled **$342,534**!

In 2005, Mr. Ellis opened a self-directed IRA and rolled over his entire 401(k) balance into his new IRA, approximately $320,000. His IRA then proceeded to purchase a used car dealership with a 98% interest in the newly formed LLC. Mr. Ellis acted as the general manager for the used-car business of which he was previously never affiliated.

Throughout 2005, Mr. Ellis received compensation from the used-car business totaling $9754 for his services as the general manager. Then, in 2006 he received an additional $29,263 for compensation. In 2005 Mr. Ellis also formed a company with his wife and three children for the purpose of purchasing rental property. One of the properties purchased was a lot that was then leased to the used car dealership.

The court ruled that the formation of the LLC with Mr. Ellis' IRA was not considered a prohibited transaction, and thus creating an LLC with retirement plan funds is not considered illegal. However, the court did find that Mr. Ellis engaged in prohibited transactions under section 4975(c)(1) (D) & (E) by paying himself a salary, which therefore caused the distribution of Mr. Ellis' IRA to become a taxable event. As such, all $321,366 of the business income was added to his personal income in 2005, which resulted in a substantial tax bill of over $130,000!

Additionally, since Mr. Ellis was not 59 ½ years old at the time of the distribution, he was required to pay an additional 10% penalty on the distribution! To compound matters even further, another 20% penalty was imposed due to negligence of the rules and regulations for paying income tax since he failed to pay anywhere close to what the full tax bill was!

In essence, Mr. Ellis conducted two specific types of prohibited transactions:

- Receiving compensation from the business funded by his IRA
- Having his personally owned rental property business to engage in business with his used-car business owned by the IRA.

For this reason and many others, it is vitally important to ensure you do not engage in self-dealing or prohibited transactions of any sort, and if at any time you find that you have made a mistake, attempt to rectify it as soon as possible. As you can see, the IRS has no mercy!

What are Prohibited Transactions?

This next section is going to talk about ways in which people violate the rules of the IRS and thereby eliminate the tax-exempt status of their retirement plans. The IRS has specific wording for this faux pas: "prohibited transactions". Quite simply, a prohibited transaction violates the rules of a qualified retirement plan by conducting transactions with unqualified individuals. As we stated in the last chapter, the purpose of having a qualified plan is to fund your future retirement. In that vein, the IRS does not want you to personally benefit from any sort of transaction that occurs prior to you taking money out as a distribution (at retirement age). Prohibited transactions are similar to self-dealing in that they do not operate within the true spirit of a qualified retirement plan.

What this means is that since you're not allowed to personally benefit from any sort of investment or transaction prior to taking the money out as a distribution, the IRS wants to make sure that you don't engage in something that might be a little bit too close to self-dealing. A prohibited transaction is one that does not occur directly with you, but rather with someone who is considered a non-qualified individual. It can also be a transaction that occurs with an entity of yours in which you could personally benefit. Could I give you anymore vague generalities? What exactly constitutes a prohibited transaction? Well, lucky for you, I have the IRS' exact wording on prohibited transactions right here:

Prohibited transactions generally include the following transactions:

- A disqualified person's transfer of plan income or assets to, or use of them by or for his or her benefit
- A fiduciary's act by which he or she deals with plan income or assets in his or her own interest
- A fiduciary's receipt of consideration for his or her own account in a transaction that involves plan income or assets from any party dealing with the plan
- Any of the following acts between the plan and a disqualified person:
- Selling, exchanging, or leasing property
- Lending money or extending credit
- Furnishing goods, services or facilities

Source: IRS.gov, Retirement Topics - Prohibited Transactions

This begs the question, who is a disqualified person? Well, again we turn to the IRS' website for the answer (don't worry; I'll break it down in a minute!)

Disqualified Person. You are a disqualified person if you are any of the following.

- A fiduciary of the plan.
- A person providing services to the plan.

157

- An employer, any of whose employees are covered by the plan.
- An employee organization, any of whose members are covered by the plan.
- Any direct or indirect owner of 50% or more of any of the following.
- The combined voting power of all classes of stock entitled to vote, or the total value of shares of all classes of stock of a corporation that is an employer or employee organization described in (3) or (4).
- The capital interest or profits interest of a partnership that is an employer or employee organization described in (3) or (4).
- The beneficial interest of a trust or unincorporated enterprise that is an employer or an employee organization described in (3) or (4).
- A member of the family of any individual described in (1), (2), (3), or (5). (A member of a family is the spouse, ancestor, lineal descendant, or any spouse of a lineal descendant.)
- A corporation, partnership, trust, or estate of which (or in which) any direct or indirect owner described in (1) through (5) holds 50% or more of any of the following.
- The combined voting power of all classes of stock entitled to vote or the total value of shares of all classes of stock of a corporation.
- The capital interest or profits interest of a partnership.
- The beneficial interest of a trust or estate.

- An officer, director (or an individual having powers or responsibilities similar to those of officers or directors), a 10% or more shareholder, or highly compensated employee (earning 10% or more of the yearly wages of an employer) of a person described in (3), (4), (5), or (7).
- A 10% or more (in capital or profits) partner or joint venturer of a person described in (3), (4), (5), or (7).
- Any disqualified person, as described in (1) through (9) above, who is a disqualified person with respect to any plan to which a section 501(c)(22) trust is permitted to make payments under section 4223 of ERISA.

Basically, you are a disqualified individual if you could potentially benefit personally from the plan, and are also somehow related or attached to the contributions of the plan. For example, your lineal descendants such as father, mother, son, daughter, and grandparents or grandchildren are disqualified. Perhaps the IRS is worried that you might want to lend money to your grandkids and then put that money in an account for "safe keeping" for them, only to be in charge of that account. Not sure if that's true, but it's illegal nonetheless. The same is true for your spouse and spouses of your lineal descendants. For some reason brothers, sisters, aunts and uncles are off the hook. Not sure why, but they are.

The fiduciary of the plan is the person or organization in charge of the safe keeping of the money within the plan. In other words, you may have $10,000 being held at an account by XYZ Company, and you cannot loan or invest in XYZ Company because they are the fiduciary of your plan. Not sure I'd want to keep my money in an organization that needs to borrow money from its plan holders anyway! (As a matter of fact, there is a court case very similar to this that resulted in unknowing customers losing upwards of $22 million to an untrustworthy custodian. Check out SEC v. American Pension Services, Inc. to learn more)

In essence you can't conduct any sort of business with any lineage or descendents so basically the vertical line on your family tree. So let's once again use real estate as an example. Let's say for example that your brother-in-law has a home that he wants to fix up and flip but he needs money in order to purchase the property and also perform the necessary repairs. He is asking for $50,000 for the repairs as well as $100,000 for the purchase. Since you have enough money in your retirement plan, and you think it's a good investment option, you can go ahead and either loan the money out to your brother-in-law for $150,000, or you could help to form a partnership with him in which you will supply the money and he will create the business. Now let's carry that example through to its conclusion. Your brother-in-law purchases the property for $100,000 and performs necessary repairs and then sells the property for $175,000. All in, the total cost was $150,000 so there is a profit of $25,000 to be realized. Depending on how you set this investment up, you can either participate in the profit that was realized from the sale of the property, or you could just be getting an investment return based on a loan that you made to your brother-in-law. Either way is completely legal as long as it is structured properly.

Here's an example of what you cannot do. Let's say we have the exact same property but it is your father who wants to purchase the property. In this case you still have the money, he still has the exact same deal, and everything else seems as though it could work right? Unfortunately, no. This would be a prohibited transaction because you're completely disallowed from investing with or loaning money to your father simply because he is a disqualified individual by nature of being your father.

Let's talk about another type of prohibited transaction, one that is very similar to self-dealing, but in essence could be considered an arm's length transaction by many novice investors. This is an actual example from a court case where investors really did lose their shirts over the entire ordeal. Let's assume you find a company, ABC Corp., that you want to purchase with your self-directed retirement plan. You have $300,000 in your plan, but the purchase price is $600,000. You know that you can't pony up the rest of the money for the purchase price because that is self-dealing and would be prohibited.

Instead, you are smart and go out and get a bank loan for the purchase of the business. Since it is an established business, you are just going to be the owner, won't receive any compensation, and in fact won't be managing the business at all. You just sign the papers from the bank for the loan, send your money from your retirement plan to the escrow company, and in the morning you wake up with a retirement plan that owns a thriving business.

Now, for fun let's say you can sell the business a few years later for $1 million! Quite a return, wouldn't you say? To keep the math simple, let's say it took five years, and you still owe $300,000 on the loan. Now, you sell the business, pay off the $300,000 bank loan, and then pay the remaining $700,000 into your retirement plan. Let's see, five years, $400,000 in profit on a $300,000 investment…that's an 18.5% annualized return tax free! Pretty awesome, don't you think?!?

Except for one minor little detail. Remember that loan you got from the bank? Well, they wouldn't let you have it unless you *personally* signed for it. What that means is you personally guaranteed the note, which means you personally involved yourself in the deal. Remember who disqualified people are? You are, for one. That means this entire deal was considered a prohibited transaction, and you now owe income taxes and penalties on your investment! In the case of Peek v. Commissioner, this resulted in over $94,000 in penalties and taxes being assessed as a result of a prohibited transaction resulting from a personal guarantee. If you don't think the IRS will notice or care about something so insignificant as who signed the dotted line, you're

162

kidding yourself!

It may seem as though there's not very much you can do with a self-directed retirement plan at this point. However, nothing could be further from the truth. The fact is that there are so many different alternative investment options available to you that being scared off by these simple prohibited transactions and self-dealing circumstances would be silly. The important point to understand is that there are rules around this type of investment plan just like there are rules around every single type of investment plan out there. The Securities and Exchange Commission regulates the financial markets, the IRS regulates the tax markets, the Department of Labor regulates the employee and employment markets, and of course the government has a hand in everything. Self-directed retirement plans are no different. They have their own regulations, and if you fail to abide by them you will be penalized.

The penalties are stiff and can range up to 150% of the transaction value, or the entire account value that you put at risk. For that reason, as well as many others, it's important to make sure that you have a good team in place to help advise you on legal and tax issues, and also to keep you educated along the way so that you don't trip up and make any mistakes. It's a good thing that you're reading this book because you'll get a lot of your questions answered before you even go talk to an advisor. In fact, it's best if you finish reading this book before you go talk to any advisors simply because most advisors will charge you a large fee regardless what questions you ask them, so be sure to get the majority of your simple questions answered by reading this book entirely, and getting further education on our website at www.AngelNetwork.com/InnerCircle before you seek out any further advice. Doing so will save you thousands of dollars, which is the topic we will talk about next.

The Pen Is Mightier...

In 2001, two individuals decided to partner up and purchase an existing company, Abbott Fire and Safety, Inc. (AFS). The two individuals, Mr. Peek and Mr. Fleck, decided to use their retirement plan balances to purchase the company. Little did they know that these purchases were going to result in over $90,000 of penalties and close to $500,000 in tax liability down the road.

Mr. Peek rolled over his previous employer's 401(k) plan into a new self-directed IRA to help fund the business. Mr. Fleck decided to do the same thing from an existing IRA he already had. In an ill-fated move, the two individuals formed FP Company on September 11, 2001 with each owning a 50% interest for a total of $309,000.

The newly formed FP Company then purchased AFS for a total of $1.1 million consisting of the following:

- $850,000 in cash derived from:
- $450,000 in a bank loan
- $400,000 from the sale of FP company stock to the IRAs
- $50,000 in the form of a promissory note to the broker
- $200,000 in the form of a promissory note to the sellers

At this point, Mr. Peek and Mr. Fleck personally guaranteed the promissory notes and secured their own personal residences as collateral for the notes. The two individuals served as officers for the new company, but don't appear to have had any active role in the operation of the organization.

In 2006, FP Company was sold for $1.67 million of which each IRA received 50% less any notes still outstanding.

Unfortunately for Mr. Peek and Mr. Fleck, the IRS reviewed their incomes tax statements for 2006 and 2007 (the two years in which the sale took place) and assessed an additional tax due to capital gains on the sale of their stock in the company. This is because the personal guarantee that was signed in 2001 invalidated the IRA at that time, and therefore all gain on the sale of the company was deemed to be a capital gain.

As a result of this ruling, the two individuals faced additional taxes of over $223,000 each, as well as more than $45,000 each in penalties! I would like to think that over $500,000 in taxes and penalties would be enough to dissuade you from conducting any illegal or prohibited transactions.

Here is the result of the penalties for the two individuals:

Taxpayers	Year	Tax Deficiency	Penalty per Section 6662(a)
Peek	2006	$223,650.00	$44,730.00
	2007	$1,399.00	$279.80
Fleck	2006	$243,229.00	$48,645.80
	2007	$4,948.00	$989.60

Just don't be *those guys!*

Part 4

Unleashing the Potential

We've now covered all the dos and don'ts of self-directed investing and the various types of plans available to you. Remember that to have a *truly self-directed* plan you must be able to invest in *any* qualified asset available on the markets, whether public or private. Many of the large investment firms will offer you a "self-directed" account, including companies such as E*TRADE, Schwab, Edward Jones, and others, but these aren't really self-directed to the extent I am talking about here. Instead, these companies just mean that you are investing without the use of a broker or advisor, and are not referring to a qualified self-directed retirement plan like I have outlined in this book.

With that being said, I'm sure you are anxious to learn the various ways by which you can start to leverage your new-found freedom with your qualified plan and start earning a return that you can brag about, right? Well, wait no longer. The remaining chapters of this book are devoted to multiplying your investments through proper investment strategies that have helped several thousand self-directed investors reap huge rewards in the past several years. Just remember to avoid the pitfalls of self-dealing or prohibited transactions mentioned in the previous section, and you should be well on your way to making a legitimate and sizable return.

As I mentioned in the opening pages of this book, I am not a subject matter expert in each area of investment. I have studied, learned, and experienced several different types of investment options available, but that by no means qualifies me to teach you on each topic. Instead, I am going to stick to educating you on areas I know and understand well. Experts in their chosen field have generously offered to provide a chapter as well to help you better understand how to invest using methods that have made them wealthy.

One other way of improving your overall rate of return is to also lower your expenses. To that end, I have engaged Karla Dennis* to provide some very valuable tax-savings advice to help you leverage your new plan and increase your wealth over the course of your lifetime. Since taxes are one area that we can neither escape from nor opt out of, it is important to know how you can reduce your taxes to the fullest extent of the law which in turn gives you more money to invest and play with. Sound good?

*Note: Karla Dennis' firm, Cohesive Tax does manage my tax plans and has proven to be a priceless resource for me personally.

The following chapters will help you to understand the realm of investing in alternative assets primarily. Many of these assets are not provided through most main stream financial firms, which are precisely what qualifies them as "alternative". You must understand that alternative assets are simply another tool you can put in your arsenal to help you improve your overall financial circumstances, but should by no means be the sole focus of your investment plan. Remember, proper diversification across several asset *classes* is what will keep you in the black. Poor diversification or venturing into unknown or unexplored investments will yield dire results.

Each of the following chapters comes with an associated audio and/or video component. Get your free copies at www.AngelNetwork.com/InnerCircle. In addition to these free resources, you can gain access to our exclusive self-directed investing coaching program and even get your own self-directed plan set up in just minutes!

Private Lending

By Richard Roop

Richard Roop is the author of "How to Make Money Working at Home as a Real Estate Investor: A Compilation of Lessons Learned from No Money Down Real Estate Investing". *Richard is considered one of the nation's best kept secrets for serious real estate investors. Sharing his Free and Clear cash strategies, Richard Roop has taught thousands of real estate investors throughout the nation how to generate cash now, cash flow, and cash for later, regardless of what's happening in the economy.*

Richard is one of the top direct response marketing 'gurus' and consultants dedicated to helping real estate investors generate more leads, negotiate better deals and create more consistent, predictable cash each month. He specializes in sharing proven, low cost real estate direct marketing strategies for attracting a steady flow of motivated sellers, as well as real estate business marketing systems for getting investment properties occupied fast.

Richard also teaches investors systematic approaches to growing their businesses, leveraging their time and increasing their profitability on each deal. His real estate direct marketing approach to investing teaches investors to achieve their financial goals WITHOUT hunting for deals, relying on agents, using their credit, offering large down payments, struggling with tenants, borrowing from banks or calling sellers.

Richard has been a full time creative real estate investor since 1996. He has bought over 500 homes, manages millions of dollars in real estate and still actively buys and sells houses every month near his home in the Woodland Park, Colorado.

Anyone looking to get a good, well-secured, higher than average return on their retirement account funds should explore and consider **private lending** to **real estate investors** as an option for their portfolio. Real estate investors seek out good deals on properties and need capital to acquire the property. They can fund the deal with their own capital, qualify for a bank loan, or get a "collateral loan" from a private lender.

Real estate investors generally pay higher interest and loan fees because they take into account these costs when making their offers to purchase, and despite these costs they expect to make a profit. They also benefit from the availability of funds to close more deals. If they relied on banks alone, the banks would place a limit on how many deals they could do thus impeding their ability to run a successful business.

Private lenders typically do not loan money based on credit, but rather based on the income and equity of the underlying collateral. This is another benefit to real estate investors; the property should be able to support the repayment of the note and offer a good cushion of equity for the lender's protection. Sufficient equity and a recorded lien on the property provide security to you as a lender. The money you invest is "secured" by equity in a property that could be sold to pay off the note.

As a private lender you loan out your investment capital to a real estate investor who wants to purchase or refinance a property, typically a single family home. It is important that any loans you do are used for business or investment purposes, and are not for owner occupants as there are very specific rules and regulations surrounding these types of loans that we won't get into here.

The borrower then executes a mortgage or deed of trust (security instrument) which is recorded on county records as a lien against the property. Clear title cannot be passed onto a buyer unless the security instrument is released. This is how a bank also secures interest in a property to ensure they are repaid when the owner sells the property. The borrower also signs a promissory note which is the promise to repay the investor. The note is an asset that your retirement account owns. It could also be sold to a note buyer as an option rather than waiting for the borrower to pay it off, typically upon the sale or refinance of the underlying collateral or property.

As an investor, you typically earn a fixed rate of annual interest on the note until it is paid off. The interest you charge is up to you and depends on what the market will bear. Real estate investors typically pay 7% to 15% interest if they know they can make a profit on their deal and get the financing quickly. As the lender, you can also charge a loan origination fee or "points". A point is 1% of the loan amount. Real estate investors typically pay 0 to 10 points in order to get their loan funded. This loan fee increases the amount of the return you get on the note above and beyond the interest charged.

Another way for a private investor to make money lending to real estate investors is by implementing a "prepayment" penalty. After going through the time and effort of closing a loan with your borrower, you may want your loan to earn interest for a minimum period of time, such as six months. If the loan is paid off within six months you might want to charge some points as a "hassle factor" since you then have to spend more time and effort reinvesting your funds. This prepayment fee ensures a minimum return is paid even if the loan is repaid very quickly. If you charge points up front as a loan origination fee, then you may not be concerned about being paid off early, and not include a prepayment penalty since you can reinvest your proceeds in another loan and collect more points.

It is important to you as a lender that you insure against possible loss. A lender's title insurance policy ensures a clear title can be transferred to a buyer, or in the case of a default, transferred to you as a lender. In the case of your borrower defaulting you may wind up with the property instead of your repayment on the note. So you never want to loan out on a property you are not willing to own. If the borrower defaults they can deed you the property instead of forcing you to foreclose to get the deed, but if they don't you will have to spend money on legal fees to go through a foreclosure procedure.

Therefore the highest amount you loan on a property should be considered based on a percentage of the property's value. This is called the "loan-to-value" or LTV. As an investor or lender, you want a cushion of equity in the property in case the real estate investor defaults and you take the property back. You would then have to resell the property to get your investment back. Most private lenders do not want to fund a loan for more than 75% of the property's value. This would be a referred to as "75% LTV".

Due to transaction costs of marketing and selling a property after repossession, you should only expect to net 80% to 90% of the property's market value when selling it. The need for an additional cushion is to protect you from market price declines, costs of repairs, and the cost of foreclosure. Therefore a maximum of 65% LTV provides even more protection.

There are several other considerations you must understand whenever creating a private loan to a real estate investor. These considerations include:

- Illiquidity
- Equity or loan to value
- Term of the loan or maturity date
- Investor's plan for repayment

- Desired return on investment or ROI
- Willingness to own the property in lieu of repayment
- Desire for cash flow or appreciation/growth
- Current property value and cost of repairs needed

When it comes to investing your retirement plan money into any investment, it is important to conduct your due diligence. This is simply an overview of how the process works. To learn more about private real estate lending and Richard Roop, go to *www.RichardRoop.com*.

Tax Savings Tips
By Karla Dennis

Karla Dennis is a tax expert and business strategist. As seen in Forbes Magazine, Karla Dennis is an expert tax and business strategist and as an enrolled agent, Karla is licensed to represent taxpayers in all 50 states. She holds a master's in taxation and business development and is the author of two books, Tax Storm and Against the Odds. Karla is a CEO of consultancy firm Cohesive, has saved her clients thousands of dollars and has been featured in various media outlets such as Forbes, MSNBC, KTLA, Yahoo Finance, and Smart Money, marking her as the ultimate tax expert. As of January of 2013, Karla became the new co-host on the Call Toni radio show, sharing her financial and business knowledge with the Greater Orange County and Los Angeles areas. As a supporter of women's rights and issues, Karla is part of the Women Network, an organization built to educate and mentor women. In addition, Karla is the radio host for Women Network Radio, a show that aims to uplift and empower women of all walks of life.

The IRS created retirement plans for two reasons. The goal was to get individuals back into investing, put some money back into the economy, back into circulation, back into investing in the marketplace, and also serve as an opportunity for individuals to have their own individual retirement accounts. A lot of companies have stopped having individual retirement accounts, and for those companies that didn't, there were people that were left out of the marketplace in terms of being able to have a retirement plan. So they created the IRA, the Individual Retirement Account, to be a supplemental way for people to save for their retirement alongside Social Security.

The IRS incentivizes people to invest in their future by giving you a tax deduction on your contributions. That's why it's called the deferred plan or "qualified money". Qualified money is money that when you set it aside it's tax-deferred, meaning you're not going to pay income taxes on it today. So the question is, do you pay income taxes in this situation on that $5,000 or you defer it and pay income taxes later on, and many people want to go the route of deferment. I'll pay the taxes when I use the money so we get that upfront tax deduction.

There are several types of plans and segregating it between individual plans and business plans is really where the difference lies. We have the individual retirement accounts (IRA) that are for the individuals who are typically W-2 employees. It's not to say if you're a business owner you can't have an IRA, but traditionally those go towards the W-2 workers who make a certain amount of money.

On the business side of the equation, they came up with the 401(k) plan, a profit-sharing plan, if you will, where employers were investing on behalf of their employees as an incentive, a benefit, and then employees then could contribute to that plan as well. Companies used to even match those dollars; some still do. So if you put in 3% of your gross salary, the company might put in 3% of your salary on your behalf.

So it's an incentive for employees to invest. But then there became the business owners who were saying, "Okay, all of these employees get these great benefits, what's out here for us that are really making this economy roar? How can we take advantage of these different things?" So then they created the 401(k) for business owners. They have the Uni-K, meaning that you don't have more than one employee, it could just be you and you can create a Solo 401(k).

They come up with the SEPs, the self-employed IRA, which is similar to the IRA but with the self-employed IRA, the SEP, you can put more money away per year. Then they come up with so many other types of retirement plans. You have the Roth that's not deferred but you have that as well, defined benefit plans. It just continues to go on and on and ever changing so business owners will invest as well.

It's really important to understand where your money is invested with these types of plans because a lot of times people think if they put their money in an IRA, that money is not necessarily invested into the marketplace, i.e. the stock market, but oftentimes it is. They feel it's a safer type of investment but it's still an investment in the marketplace and it's an opportunity to participate in a more controlled environment, and it is also is a kick starter for the economy. Our government always wants money moving in the economy to further the economy and further jobs and growth. That is the main purpose behind having retirement plans invested into the public markets.

One of the benefits of having a robust economy is that everyone has an income, taxes are being paid, and people are generally happy. For this reason, the government also encourages people to start and operate businesses. When someone goes into business, they're in business to earn a decent wage for the skill they know, and to also earn a profit. Most of us that are business owners have a skill and we could probably go out into the marketplace and work for someone else. So that's our wage. That's our earning for our skill. But when you start a business, you need to really get that leverage to make a profit as well as earnings on your wages. One way to earn a profit in a business is to reduce your taxes, which are sometimes the single biggest expense for new business owners.

Most business owners have a skill, go out and hang their shingle and become a sole proprietor by default. As a sole proprietor business or if you're looking at a Limited Liability Company and you are a single member of that company, you automatically default back to a sole proprietor business, which means that you're going to file a business return, a Schedule C, with your personal income tax return. Those types of businesses are subject to self-employment tax. Any net profit from that business is subject to self-employment tax and that self-employment tax rate is currently 15.3%. Most employees that are converted into a business owner are used to having their employer pay half of their self-employment tax. They'll see withholdings on their paycheck, Social Security, Medicare and whatever their tax withholdings are, but they don't see the full impact of the tax because they're only paying half. When you become self-employed, you're responsible for the full payment, which is why a retirement plan becomes even more significant because when you set aside dollars into your retirement plan, depending on how you do that, those dollars can be excluded from some of those taxes. It really is going to lower your overall income tax bill and really help you be able to pay the taxes you need to pay.

Setting up the right structure from the beginning is incredibly important. It's really about taking the time to plan. If you don't take the time to plan, you plan to fail. And that's where I'm really a big advocate of sitting down and trying to envision your bigger picture. You may not be there yet but every business owner who starts a business has a goal in mind, and they may have not put that goal down on paper but it's certainly in their heads. Many of their goals are very ambitious and very doable. So the way that I like to look at it is, "what is your big picture?" Then let's reverse-engineer the proper entity you should be in.

Personally, for me, I don't recommend my clients go into sole proprietorships just because I don't know any business that wants to pay a tremendous amount of taxes nor do I know any business that wants to keep having to switch out bank accounts when you incorporate and change things around. As a smart strategic business person, you really want to set yourself up to be the business you want to become.

We don't want overkill, but certainly if you're looking to be a business owner, you are probably looking to make money.

So if you want to make money, make a profit, you have to think in terms of protecting that profit from the very beginning and not wait until the profit gets there and go, "Oops, I'm going to have to pay a tremendous amount in taxes. What do I do now?" One way to ensure you are saving money on your taxes is to have the right type of retirement plan in place from the very beginning, and structure your business in a manner that will save you money on taxes for years to come.

Karla Dennis' company, Cohesive Tax, is located in Cypress, CA and specializes in helping people and businesses with their accounting and tax planning needs. To hear the full interview with Karla, and to learn more about how you can work with Karla directly to minimize your taxes and get the most income out of your job or business through proper planning and setup, go to www.AngelNetwork.com/InnerCircle.

Private Partnerships, Businesses, and Equity Investing

This is actually an area that I, Jeff Barnes, am very excited about, and love talking to people about. I have raised money through private placement memorandums (PPM) and really enjoy the art of making private deals for businesses and equity investments. There is so much to cover in this area that it is impossible to cover it all in just a few short pages. Instead, I want you to visit our resource page: www.AngelNetwork.com/InnerCircle to get a greater understanding of how this world works.

To say that private equity investing is complicated is an understatement. In fact, there are complete sections of the SEC codes that regulate private investing in general which can cause anyone trying to raise money serious heartburn. Section 506 of the SEC discusses at great length how private equity investing works. The term "private equity" simply refers to having an equity (ownership) position in a private company. Many people might refer to these as private partnerships, non-public investments or offerings, or several derivatives thereof.

There are generally three different ways for an investor to partake in private equity deals. These are:

- Angel Investing

- Venture Capital

- Syndication

For simplicity's sake, we are only going to discuss angel investing here. Venture capitalists are generally firms made up of several wealthy individuals or families who invest in the $5 million and up range. If you are a VC reading this, then by all means hit me up and we'll get some great deals going! Most likely VC's (not Viet Cong) will not need retirement funds to get funding, but rather use pensions and financial institutions to fund large (or potentially large) businesses. Think Google, Facebook, Tesla, etc. before they went public.

Syndication is simply a way for multiple investors to pool their money into one fund in order to buy a company, property, or other investment. Syndication is used often in the commercial real estate world where large chunks of capital are needed to purchase a single building. The process of syndicating funds can be complex and will be discussed further on your included membership site at www.AngelNetwork.com/InnerCircle.

The most often used and powerful way (in my opinion) for small time investors to invest is through Angel investing. Angel investing consists of basically buying up a small portion of a startup business when the company needs capital the most. These companies have already gotten started but need to expand, hire, or in some way put capital to use to build upon their early success. Angels come in to provide money to entrepreneurs up to about $1 million. Think ABC's Shark Tank.

Angel investing is something that can be very fun and very lucrative for investors with a reasonable net worth and money to invest. These are generally accredited investors who meet the following requirements:

- Net worth over $1 million excluding personal residence
- Income over $300,000 in the past two years as a married couple (with a reasonable expectation of making that again in the foreseeable future)
- Income over $200,000 as a single investor

The reason Angel investors are generally accredited investors is due to the SEC requirements I mentioned earlier. In many cases it can be difficult to raise money from non-accredited investors simply due to these regulations. Therefore, if you are investing in a small company and are not accredited, you will want to conduct further due diligence and ensure an attorney is hired to draft the agreements when you invest. The last thing you want is for your money to be invested with little or no chance of getting it back.

Like I said, private equity investing is a rather long and complex topic that could take a long time to get through. For that reason, I have included a section entirely devoted to private equity investing at www.AngelNetwork.com/InnerCircle for your viewing pleasure.

However, I want to give you one very "prime time" example of how powerful having a truly self-directed retirement plan, coupled with private equity investing can really pay off. If you remember the former presidential hopeful Mitt Romney, then you might remember a lot of hullabaloo surrounding is astronomical IRA balance.

Romney stated during his presidential run that his IRA was worth approximately $102 Million! Now, for most people this is unconceivable, including many of his peers and colleagues. However, there is a very real way in which Romney could have achieved this incredible account balance. One such method is through utilizing what is called "carried interest", which is simply a portion of the profit realized on private equity deals. In the private equity world, general partners generally invest a portion of their own money along with their firm's money during a leveraged buyout.

The proceeds of these investments are generally a fraction of the overall deal. William Cohan of *The Atlantic* lays out a compelling case where Romney could have invested $30,000 from his self-directed retirement plan into a deal that was worth approximately $500 Million. In this situation, the $30,000 was a small portion of what the partners at Romney's firm was required to put up, but since he was the founder of the company, he would receive one-third of the profits generated on the deal. All in, the private equity firm would likely have put in $100

Million from the company itself, as well as the partners.

If the company that the equity firm purchased was later sold for $1 Billion, as in Cohan's example, then the proceeds would play out like this:

	Amount
Proceeds from Sale	$1,000,000,000
Less Debt Payoff	$400,000,000
Remaining Profit	$600,000,000
20% Split to Partners	$120,000,000
80% Split for Company	$480,000,000
Romney's Third of Partner Share	$40,000,000
Remaining Partners Share	$80,000,000

As you can see, Romney could very well have put up $30,000 into a private equity deal worth $500 Million initially. If the company doubled in value and was sold for $1 Billion, then the amount Romney put in via is retirement plan would be returned in proportion to the agreement made during the initial investment. The challenge here is, why would someone want to do this and get $40 Million in a retirement plan they can't touch until they are 59 ½, and will then have to pay ordinary income taxes on the distribution?

Well, what if Romney had a Roth plan when he made the initial investment? In this case, the return on his investment is not only astronomical, but it is also tax-free! Another great provision about the Roth plan is that the initial contributions can be withdrawn at any time without penalty. The investment returns cannot be withdrawn without penalty until the age of 59 ½, but the contributions can.

Although this is an incredibly unusual example of how a self-directed retirement plan can be used with private investing, it is very clear that it is possible. After all, a person vying for the top position in our country utilized strategies outlined in this book to amass the wealth of a small country in a tax-deferred retirement plan! If it worked for him, I'm guessing you can make it work for yourself too!

Summary

You now understand what self-directed investment plans are and how powerful they can be for your future retirement. There are two primary types of retirement plans that I discussed in this book, but you can also self-direct other types of plans with the right setup. We do not advocate any one specific investment option or investment decision at our company. However, we strongly advocate the use of a self-directed retirement plan to help you on the path to true retirement riches. It's important to understand that the traditional model of retirement planning and investing is heavily weighted in favor of the investment firms who offer these plans. The goal of investing is to benefit your future self and family, and to help you be one of the people who can truly say they don't need a handout to survive.

It is important to understand that you have options when it comes to retirement planning. As with anything, making the right choice today will lead to happiness and fulfillment down the road. However, making the wrong choice or not making any choice at all leaves you vulnerable to risks beyond your control and jeopardizes your financial future and wellbeing. The choice is yours to make, so be sure to choose wisely.

Throughout this book you have been offered a chance to get more training and access to a wide array of education, products, and services that will help you on your path to financial freedom. I encourage you to go to www.AngelNetwork.com/InnerCircle to learn more about these resources available to you. Some resources will require additional investment, but there are many that are still free and easy to use and digest. It is important that you do something at this point, even if it means reading and learning more to determine if this is even the right course for you. What you don't want to do is simply put down this book and say, "Well, that was nice," and leave it at that.

The world has changed. The economy has changed. Investing has become more complex. However, the basic tenets of investing remain the same, and through proper planning and concentrated efforts of study, you too can reach your financial goals sooner than you thought possible!

ABOUT THE AUTHOR

As a U.S. Navy submariner, Jeff Barnes traveled the world underwater at extreme depths, running a nuclear power plant and sleeping with torpedoes while learning invaluable skills. His innate leadership ability and understanding of complex systems allowed him to run the largest division on his submarine and take charge of the ship's quality control program.

After an honorable discharge from the Navy, Jeff took his expertise and experience to corporate America, helping clients grow their businesses as a risk management consultant while also coaching and consulting small business owners on the side.

This led to Jeff running his own division inside a Fortune 500 company focused on technology and innovation, leading multiple international innovation projects and bringing new products and services to the global market. As a result of this exposure, Jeff has given training to thousands of executives on how to utilize technology and innovation to grow a business.

As an entrepreneur himself and a best-selling author, Jeff has trained, coached, and consulted with hundreds of entrepreneurs and business owners to implement complex growth systems to help them grow their companies quickly and make a positive impact on the world.

This led to Jeff becoming the CEO for Angel Investors Network, an organization helping entrepreneurs achieve their dreams since 1997. In this role he works with A-list business executives and celebrities such as Steve Forbes of Forbes Media, Kevin Harrington from ABC's Shark Tank, the co-founder of Whole Foods John Mackey, and many others. Jeff continues helping entrepreneurs find the investors and funding they need to scale their businesses fast, and acts as a preliminary judge on Angel Investors Network's "Pitch Tank" – a live Shark Tank style event hosted in front of thousands of investors (www.ThePitchTank.com).

Jeff spends a great deal of time coaching his two boys' sports teams and traveling. Jeff continues traveling the world speaking and finding great places for scuba diving, a skill he gained as a former U.S. Navy scuba diver. Jeff's love for the outdoors, camping, diving, the environment and helping others earned him a seat on the board of Lifeschool, a nonprofit organization helping under-privileged youth gain skills they don't learn in school.

Jeff has a passion for helping people to leave a financial legacy for their family for generations to come. If you are interested in learning how to work directly with Jeff on your personal financial goals and objectives, or are interested in taking control of your financial future, visit www.AngelNetwork.com/InnerCircle to get more information.

Additional References

Department of Labor. (2010, 10 20). *Fiduciary Requirements for Disclosure in Participant-Directed Individual Account Plans.* Retrieved 2014, from Federal Register: https://webapps.dol.gov/FederalRegister/HtmlDisplay.aspx?DocId=24323&AgencyId=8&DocumentType=2

Hiltonsmith, R. (2010). *The Retirement Savings Drain.* New York: Demos.

Investment Company Institute. (2014). *2013 Investment Company Fact Book.* Washington DC: Investment Company Institute.

Terry L Ellis and Sheila K Ellis, Petitioners V. Commissioner of Internal Revenue, Respondent, 12960–11 (United States Tax Court October 29, 2013).

United States Code. (2012, January 3). *15 U.S.C. 80B-5 - INVESTMENT ADVISORY CONTRACTS.* Retrieved 2014, from US Government Printing Office: http://www.gpo.gov/fdsys/granule/USCODE-2011-title15/USCODE-2011-title15-chap2D-subchapII-sec80b-5